CW00429624

Table of Contents

Acknowledgements

Many people have played a positive role in my life, but there is space here to thank only a few. A number of people contributed to making my childhood less damaging that it would otherwise have been. I would like to thank Beryl and Tony, our neighbours, who were there for us for years, every time we needed help. Thanks also to my childhood friend Elizabeth and her family; you were truly amazing, and I will never forget the laughs we shared. Love and thanks to Lee, my best friend in childhood, and to his family. Lee, you were with me on my journey, you were always there for me when I needed something, and you never judged me. I miss you loads.

To the many schoolmates who bullied me when we were all young and foolish – I forgive you, and I wish you all the best with your lives.

Thank you to the many friends I have made over the years.

Thank you to Anne, who gave me so much support when I needed it most, and to Mark and Angie, Connor and Deana – you are all truly amazing!

My thanks and love to my husband, Tony, who saw something in me that I could not have possibly seen on my own, for never turning your back on me, for making me the person I am today, and for supporting me in writing this book.

To our son: I promise you that I will always be there for you, I will love you unconditionally, and I will support you through life's journey.

Foreword

Murder, trust, betrayal, and disbelief; four words that can help us to gain insight into the life and experience of Nick Castree.

I had heard of the disappearance and discovery of Lesley Molseed, not at the time of her tragic death, but years later, when I first joined the Prison Service and encountered Stefan Kiszko, the man wrongfully convicted and eventually released after his appeal. Stefan served 16 years for a crime he hadn't committed. Lesley had, in fact, been murdered by someone else; Ronald Castree, whom I also encountered during my 25-year career in some of the country's most notorious prisons.

Following the murder of my daughter, Nicola, in 2012 (Nicola was a police officer who lost her life alongside her colleague in an appalling gun and grenade attack in Manchester), I established a charity in her name to help the families left behind after losing a loved one to murder. My work involved contact with police officers at different events. Following the horrific terrorist attack in Manchester in 2017, I met Nick, a police officer's partner, and we started to discuss how murder impacts families. Then he told me that Ronald Castree was his father. This was something totally different for me. I had met people who had committed the horrific act of murder, and I had met the families of murder victims after becoming one myself. I had never met a murderer's son.

Most people, if their father had committed such an evil act and enjoyed freedom for so long, knowing that an innocent man had been locked up, would choose to withdraw and probably feel ashamed, as if they too were responsible. Nick has chosen to react differently. After all, he wasn't responsible for the actions of his father, all those years ago. Instead, he has chosen to tell his story of how he suffered years of abuse and could very easily have suffered a fate like Lesley's. Nick could quite easily have withdrawn into a "normal" life with a partner and child, never to speak of his life growing up, trusting the father who betrayed him with his dark secrets, the grandfather who abused him, and the others he allowed into his life. Instead, he has decided to tell his story in this book, giving the reader insights into the life of a young boy trusting and being betrayed by those close to him. His book is an emotional journey about how someone can choose to pick themselves up and strive to be an "ordinary" person with a "normal" life, despite awful circumstances.

Bryn Hughes

Chapter One: The Beginning of the End

Memory is by definition subjective, and this book is based on my personal memories. I recognise that some of the people mentioned may remember some things differently. I wish them no harm with my account, which is as true as subjective memory allows, and I wish them the best in their lives.

It was the morning after Bonfire Night, 2006, and I had no reason to expect that this was going to be anything but a very ordinary day. I had worked on the night shift at the local old people's home, about ten minutes away from the apartment I shared with my partner, Tony. I had always loved my work, but it could be tiring and draining, dealing with people with dementia and other problems, and I was looking forward to getting back to my own place, kicking off my shoes and crawling into bed. Tony and I lived in an apartment in an old, converted mill, and I loved it. For me, our apartment had always been a real refuge from the stress and hustle of everyday life; a place where nobody and nothing could hurt me, because here I was safe. Life was great for me then. I enjoyed my work, I had no financial worries, and today, like every day, I was going home to the person I love most of all.

On the streets of Rossendale, there had been an air of excitement all week as all the local kids enjoyed the chaos that Bonfire Night always brings. They had been getting ready for it for days, and the uproar had come to a head the night before. It was all good fun for the kids, but the fireworks that had been exploding intermittently all day had made a lot of the home's residents nervous and restless. As the evening grew dark, they had enjoyed looking out their windows at the coloured lights against the wintry sky as they sipped their mugs of Horlicks and snuggled into their blankets and slippers, but the associated booms and blasts also reminded them of the war and sparked off memories of rationing, bombing raids, and a very different time in their lives. One of the residents even remembered the First World War. They all started recalling days when they had been young and fit and active, and the future had been bright. Many had responded to this flood of memories and emotion by becoming agitated and difficult, and we had had to work hard to calm ruffled nerves and get everyone quiet and ready for bed. It had been a more demanding shift than usual, and now I was ready for bed, too.

I opened the door quietly. Tony, a police officer, had finished his night shift just before me, and he was already in bed and drifting off. I brushed my teeth, undressed, and crawled in beside him. Tony opened one eye when he felt me turn down the duvet.

"Are you OK, Tricky?" he muttered sleepily.

"Tricky" is Tony's pet name for me because he says that he always has to figure out what I really mean when I tell him things. He extended one arm and patted me on the head.

"Fine. More than ready for some shut-eye."

Tony fell back to sleep straight away, but I have never been a good sleeper and I lay under the duvet feeling both exhausted and restless. Just as I began drifting towards unconsciousness, I heard the intercom buzzer ring. I ignored it, rolled over, and closed my eyes. We had been invited to a party for Tony's niece and nephew later that day, and I wanted to be well-rested so that I could enjoy the fun.

The intercom rang again.

Bloody hell, I thought. *Trick and treating should be over by now. It's Bonfire Night, not Hallowe'en. And it's nearly the bloody morning. Stupid kids.*

I knew that none of our friends or family would come to visit at this time, especially when Tony and I were both on night shift and needed our rest. I assumed it was some of the local children, reluctant to admit that Bonfire Night was over for another year. I closed my eyes even tighter and tried to will the noise to stop.

The buzzer continued to ring imperiously. I was awake now, and I knew that I wasn't going to get back to sleep unless I could get it to stop. Cursing under my breath, I crawled out of bed and made my way to the CCTV monitor. I was furious by now, and prepared to read the riot act to whoever had the temerity to stop me from getting my precious sleep. I looked at the monitor, expecting to see some kids in hoodies trying to make Bonfire Night last for just another couple of hours. Instead, the visitors were two adults; a smartly dressed man and woman. They seemed quite sure that someone must be home, and to have no intention of going anywhere until they had been let in. Immediately, I knew that something was wrong and, although I had no specific reason to be concerned about anything, I started to tremble.

I pushed a button on the intercom.

"This is Nick. Who is that, please?"

The man looked directly at the monitor. His expression was serious and unsmiling.

"Nick, we're police officers from the West Yorkshire Police Child Protection Unit. Can we come in and have a word, please?"

I pressed the buzzer down and held it so that the door would open, and the pair disappeared from view. I knew that they were on their way upstairs to speak to me. I felt weak as I continued to stand there with my hand on the intercom. Police officers! I wondered what they could be doing here. Had I done something wrong? I knew that I hadn't, but I couldn't stop myself from scanning through the last few days at work, just in case I had been accused of behaving inappropriately in any way. Any man working in a caring profession knows that, because he works with vulnerable people in a society in which women are seen as the natural nurturers, there are still many who find it odd for him to take on that role. Ask any male nurse or childminder; they're all extremely careful not to do anything that could be misinterpreted. At work, I had never tried to hide the fact that I am a gay man. Why should I? I had also been very aware of the fact that it was always hugely important to behave professionally and appropriately with the vulnerable people in my care. For me, this was even more important than it is for most men in my field, because Tony is a ranking police officer with the Manchester Police Force, and if I was ever accused of being less than professional, this would affect him, too. But we'd all heard the stories of men who had been falsely accused of inappropriate behaviour. Even when they've been found innocent of all blame, their careers and lives have been destroyed. People say that there's no smoke without fire and that they must have done something to deserve the shadow of suspicion. Many of them never work again.

By the time the police officers arrived at my apartment, my heart was pounding in my chest. I opened the door and let them in. Very politely, they thanked me, introduced themselves, and showed me their identification. They didn't leave me in suspense for very long.

"Nicholas," the woman said, quite gently. "We are very sorry to have to tell you this, but we have arrested your father, Ronald Castree, on suspicion of the murder of Lesley Molseed."

She looked at me. Neither her face nor her expression revealed any particular emotion. She was just doing her job.

"I'm not surprised," I blurted out.

I didn't know exactly what I was feeling in that moment. Time warped. I could see the police officers looking at me, assessing my reaction. My legs began to buckle, and I sank into the settee. My mind was numb and blank, but my body and instincts took over. I began shaking uncontrollably and weeping like a child.

Lesley Molseed. How well I knew that name. She had died in 1975, a full four years before I was born, but people in our area had still talked about her when I was a child.

A little girl of ten, small and delicate for her age because she had a history of ill-health, and vulnerable because of her mild learning disability and trusting nature, the defenceless Lesley had been raped and murdered, thrown away like a broken toy. Her mum had sent her out to the shops to run a few errands, but Lesley had never come home, and her little body had been found on the moor, covered in stab wounds. My mother had been in hospital recovering from health complications she had developed while giving birth to my older brother Jason at the time, but even she had followed the case from her bed. It was in all the papers. Lesley would have found it difficult to know whom to trust. Someone had taken advantage of her innocence in the worst possible way. When I was growing up, all the mothers used to warn their kids about speaking to strange men: "You don't want to end up like poor little Lesley Molseed, do you?"

"What the bloody hell is going on?"

It was Tony. He was in his pyjamas, his hair tousled. He took in the bizarre scene. I was huddled on a corner of the settee, crying like a child, and the police officers were standing in our living room, wondering what they should do next.

"They've just arrested my dad for Lesley Molseed's murder," I managed to tell him. "And I'm sure he's the one who did it."

"Bloody hell." Tony sat down. "I remember the case," he told the officers. "I'm in the job as well."

Tony was telling them that he was also a member of the Force.

The police officers started to explain a few things, slipping into jargon because they knew that Tony would understand what they were saying. They explained that Lesley's killer had ejaculated on her underwear at the time of her murder. Her clothing had been retained as evidence after her tiny body was found discarded on Saddleworth Moor with twelve stab wounds, one of which penetrated her heart. She was still fully dressed, but someone had arranged her body in a pose and ejaculated on her, before leaving her small frame discarded on the ground like the leftovers of a picnic. In 1975, when Lesley died, DNA testing was not yet available, but someone had the forward thinking to retain a sample of the semen in conditions good enough to preserve the DNA. They must have hoped that one day it could be tested. Finally, it had been, and the evidence proved that the ejaculate belonged to my father, and not Stefan Kiszko, the man who had served most of his adult life for a crime he had nothing to do with. Kiszko had been released in the early 1990s, when it emerged that he couldn't have left semen on Lesley's clothing because a medical condition meant that he was incapable of producing sperm, and when some girls who had testified against him, saying that he was a pervert who had exposed himself to them, admitted that they had made it all up. Dad's DNA was on file because he had been accused of committing a violent rape in 2005. He had been in a hotel room with a prostitute who left the room screaming and in tears, accusing him of having raped her. The police were called to the scene and Dad was arrested, but he was never formally charged and the case did not go to trial. The police told us that this was because of doubts about the woman's state of mental health, and fears that it was pointless to take the case, as she would not be a reliable witness. Even if they thought he had done it, it would have been impossible to prove.

Nowadays, it's illegal to retain DNA samples from anyone who has not been proven guilty of a crime. Fortunately, this decision was not taken until after Dad had been obliged to provide a sample. Even without this evidence, I knew that Dad was more than capable of killing Lesley Molseed. I knew that he was guilty. On some level, I had always known what he was capable of.

"Excuse me for a minute."

I got up and went to the bathroom. I stood in front of the sink and looked at my tear-stained, swollen face in the mirror. Everything was the same. But, at the same time, everything was utterly different. Yesterday, I'd been a bloke who had overcome a difficult childhood to find personal and professional happiness with the man I love. Today, I was the son of a paedophile and a murderer. Was I about to lose everything?

***

Never talk to strange men. Like every mother, that's what Mum always told me and my brothers. She wanted us to stay safe, even if she was no longer – or had never been – able to take care of herself. None of us knew that the bogeyman she warned us about was actually the husband and father who shared our house.

I was born on the second of June, 1979, to my dad, Ronald Castree, and my mum, Beverly. Mum had been in labour since the day before, although as my older brother Jason had been induced, she hadn't realised what was going on when she started getting cramps. By the time Mum knew what was happening, the labour was quite advanced, and she was scared, as she had been told that it was going to be a breech birth and she knew that meant that the level of risk was higher. From the start, I haven't been one to do what he is told! Dad tried to arrange an ambulance, and then a police escort, but in the end, he had to drive Mum to St Mary's Hospital in Manchester on his own. Whenever she told me the story of my birth, Mum stressed how frightened she had been, as Dad veered dangerously around corners, ran through red lights, and generally risked both their lives in his efforts to get her to the hospital as quickly as possible. I was born feet first to an audience of medical students, anxious to see a breech birth for themselves. Despite Mum's fears, I was a normal, healthy baby and gave no particular cause for concern.

Dad was a comic book salesman with a sideline in smutty magazines, up to and including hardcore porn, and the business was in a permanent state of near bankruptcy. Dad had a privileged background, and had been given a private education, and had parents who were on first name terms with some of the most influential people in their hometown of Rochdale, such as Cyril Smith, the MP. He had been sent to piano lessons and taught everything he needed to know to fit in with the moneyed middle classes. When he left school, he went straight into a career in accounts. Somehow, however, things had never worked out that well for him professionally, and the main point of the comic book shop seemed to be to surround him with kids spending their pocket money. There was never enough money to go around. As it didn't really make any difference whether he worked or not, Dad took a week off when I was born. The idea had been that he would help out at home and take care of Jason, my older brother, while Mum recovered from the birth, but Dad had always hated housework, feeling that it was beneath him and, as Mum remembered it, he caused more trouble than anything else.

When I was five weeks old, the Rochdale police arrested Dad and a friend of his, Andrew Muircroft, in connection with a robbery at International Metals Rochdale, where Dad had a part time job as an Administration Manager. Two thousand pounds had been stolen. The robbery had apparently taken place while Dad was on his way back from the bank with the company's money. Later on, Mum heard that the alleged robbers had held Dad at gunpoint and raced off towards the motorway, taking the money with them. The police searched the whole house to see if the money was there. They didn't find it and Dad was never charged, as they never found any evidence against him. Of course, I don't remember the robbery and Dad's arrest, but I do remember how it was frequently referenced whenever Mum and Dad had one of their fights, which were regular occurrences throughout my childhood, and generally ended when Dad started putting up his fists and beating Mum. On the night of his arrest, Dad had collapsed and had required medical attention when he came home from the police station. He had been taken to Oldham Boundary Park Hospital with internal injuries and broken ribs. Dad always said that the police had beaten him up in an attempt to get a confession out of him. I have often wondered if they suspected more about him than they were letting on.

***

I was one of three boys: Jason, me and Daniel, in order of age. Although he didn't know it yet, Jason, my older brother, was the only one not biologically related to Dad, having been conceived during a break in Mum and Dad's relationship when she had an affair with a married man. The man wanted nothing to do with his son, but Mum would always remember him as having been the love of her life. Because my grandmother – Nan – had always disliked Dad, Jason was her firm favourite because she saw Daniel and me as extensions of our father. While I can't blame Nan for despising her son-in-law, it was hard on me and Daniel. It wasn't our fault.

I was quite fond of my paternal grandparents. They had a comfortable house in Rochdale, and my grandmother was a real lady. She didn't have the flat regional accent that most of the people in the area do, but cut-glass tones that made me think of the old TV show *Upstairs Downstairs*. She was always impeccably dressed, and we were all impressed by her connections with some of the most influential people in the area. Grandma's father had owned a chain of tobacconists and done quite well for himself, leaving her with a private income. She was somewhat distant but quite kind to us kids, and I remember enjoying baking with her. Grandad was often upstairs in his room resting, because he had a bad back.

When we had finished baking and were waiting for the fairy buns to cool, I used to play with my toy cars while Grandma and Mum had a chat. Although Grandma was Dad's mother, sometimes Mum would complain about him, because he had been hitting her or not giving her enough money for the housekeeping.

"It's just hard," she would say. "I have three children to look after, and Ron doesn't accept how much it costs to run a household. Sometimes I have to get the children clothes, which means that there's less money for food. And then he gets so angry, and I am scared that he might hurt them…"

Grandma would make sympathetic noises and make Mum tea, and then she would give her advice.

"Look Bev, don't make a fuss," she would say. "Ronnie didn't mean it. Try to keep calm for the sake of the kids. You know he really loves you. It's just the way he is. Did you do anything to provoke him?"

Mum was always talked around and, when we were leaving, Gran would press some money into her hand to help with the housekeeping, or so that she could do her nails and look prettier so that Dad wouldn't get so annoyed the next time. Grandma always left Mum feeling that, whatever had happened, it was probably her fault.

Because Mum had only been sixteen when she and Dad got together, eighteen when they married, and had fallen quickly under the influence of her domineering husband, even though he was just two years older than her, she was very immature in many respects. She lacked confidence, because she had not had the opportunity to grow up on her own, and because she lived with a man who told her every day that she was a stupid, useless cow, and that nobody else would want her. That she was lucky he put up with her, so she'd better stick with him and try to keep him happy or she might find herself out on the streets. With her long dark hair and big eyes, Mum was pretty, but she would never have believed it. Mum may well have wished in the years to come that she had never returned to the man who beat, abused, and raped her. But if she hadn't, then I would never have been born, and nor would Daniel. With three young children to care for by the time she was in her late twenties, she must have felt that there was no way out.

Our home was an ordinary two-up three-down terrace of the sort you'll see in any British city or town. At the front, it gave onto the road, and there was just a small backyard, so we usually played indoors. I loved my older brother, Jason, and always tried to be just like him, often to his great irritation. Daniel, born five years after me, tagged along behind both of us. Photos from the time show me as a blond, blue-eyed child in dungarees, with a mischievous twinkle in my eye. Daniel was even blonder, a dead-ringer for the Milky Bar kid, and Jason was dark.

I remember how suddenly the atmosphere at home would change when Dad walked in the door in the evening. One minute, Jason and I would be playing soldiers, or we would be on the living room floor playing happily with our toys while little Daniel gurgled contently in his pram, and then the door would open and Dad would storm in. All activity would cease as the family held its collective breath, waiting to see what sort of mood Dad was in. If he had had a bad day at the shop, he would take it out on the whole family, starting before the door had even finished closing. If he had had a good day, we might just get to play a little longer before the shouting started. The only time he was ever kind was when he took us to Centre Parcs on holiday and tried to teach us how to swim. Everyone thought he was great fun, because he told the other parents that he was happy to teach their kids, too. The only happy memories I have are of being on holiday, and that is just because we were away from our house.

Because she knew what her husband was like, Mum always had a meal ready for Dad and she would offer it to him as soon as he got back to the house in the evening. This was another tense moment. As often as not, Dad would look at the meal, wrinkle his nose in disgust, and then pick up the plate and fling it violently against the kitchen wall.

"I'm not eating that fucking muck!" Dad would shout. "You can't do anything right. You can't cook right. You can't even get anything right. You're a useless fucking excuse for a woman. I work my fingers to the bone for you and your brats; the least I should expect is a decent fucking meal when I get home."

At that, Mum would usher the kids out and tell us to play upstairs. As we trailed upstairs on the way to our room, we would hear the shouting continue.

"You're a lousy bloody wife," Dad would yell. "You're not fit to be married to me. I work all the hours in the day to take care of you and your brats and you can't even cook me a decent meal!"

"I'm sorry, Ronald," Mum would say. For a while, she would try to placate him. That never worked. Then she would try to give him some of his own medicine. "You're nothing but a bully!" she would shout. "You're behaving like a brute, like you always do, and I'm going to go back to my mother! I don't deserve to live like this. I'm a good person."

"Do then," he invariably responded. "Get the hell out and take the bloody kids with you, because I sure as heck don't want them. How do I know if they are even mine? Your oldest whelp bloody isn't, you whore."

Then Mum would come upstairs with her latest bruise already swelling on her face.

"Pack your things, boys," she would say, "because we're going to stay at Nan's for a while."

By the time I was six, I understood that Mum's tears were often related to the fact that Dad saw other women and gave them the money she needed for us and the house. I didn't know what the word "sex" meant, but I knew that it had something to do with it. Every time Mum and Dad had an argument, the next day he would go and find another woman and take her to a hotel. Hotels, I learned, were expensive, and a week's housekeeping could easily go on a single night. It was easy for Dad to meet women because of his shop or his stand in the market where he sold his wares, and because there were lots of women who would "do anything" for twenty quid, including things that most women would balk at.

My heart always sank when Mum got out the laundry basket and started going through the dirty clothes, because doing the laundry always ended up with her in tears. Mum would go through Dad's pockets and find women's telephone numbers scrawled on crumpled pieces of paper, and little shiny packets with the corners torn off. She would confront Dad with this evidence of his infidelities when he got home from work, and he would slap her in the face and tell her that she deserved whatever she got. Once she found a credit card she didn't know he had.

"What's this, Ron?" Mum yelled when he got home, brandishing the credit card. "Are you using this on your tarts while your kids have to make do in hand-me-downs?"

"It's none of your fucking business, that's what it is," Dad said. "Why isn't my dinner on the table, you lazy, fat-arsed bitch?"

The more money Dad spent on his mysterious women, the harder it was for Mum to keep things ticking over at home. In order to finance his girlfriends and habit of visiting prostitutes, we had to go without clean clothes and fresh fruit and vegetables, the house was an absolute wreck, and Mum seemed to be almost always on the verge of tears. When Princess Diana gave her famous interview about her marriage, saying that there had always been a third person in it, that sounded very familiar to me. The big difference was that the third party in Mum and Dad's marriage was a series of prostitutes and women down on their luck, rather than someone he actually loved.

Although she seemed to hate Daniel and me, Nan – Mum's mother – was kind in some ways. She tried to support her daughter, but she was from the generation that believed that marriage was not to be taken lightly, and as she had worked all her life, she could be impatient with Mum and what looked like her choice to be a full-time wife and mother. Nan told Mum that she had made her bed, and now she had to lie in it, but when things got really bad, she would let Mum take us kids around to her place and stay there until things calmed down. We would stay for a few days, and then go back home again. Dad would be all right at first, even a bit apologetic sometimes, but a few days later it would be more of the same. I had a small Thomas the Tank Engine case, and I was very accustomed to packing it with my few bits and pieces and my little toothbrush so that we could all go to spend the night at Nan's. Sometimes we would go to stay with our Auntie Enid in Morecambe. Auntie Enid was really Mum's uncle's wife and our great aunt by marriage. She and Uncle Jack were kindness personified. They opened their big, detached house to us and made us feel welcome. I remember that they had a red Austin Allegro car which, to us, seemed the height of sophisticated motoring.

Of course, we never stayed at Nan's or Auntie Enid's for long, because Dad always turned up insisting that he was sorry, that it would never happen again, and that if Mum would just trust him this last time and come back home he would be a reformed character, and we would all live happily ever after. Mum wanted to believe this fairy story so much, she always went back to him – and as she had little work experience, she had no confidence in her ability to get a job and support us if she ever left.

We children were all accident prone and we made many trips to the hospital to be patched up. Jason had a big, metal tipper truck. It was bright yellow and shiny, and as soon as Jason had grown too big to want to play with it, I was delighted to assume possession. The truck was so big that a small boy could actually sit on it, and I promptly rode it down a steep hill, only to find myself heading in one direction and the truck in another. I had to be taken to hospital to have my split head sewn back together. Many more accidents followed as, like most boys, I enjoyed rough and tumble games and loved to climb trees, among other things. I have a lot of memories of being taken to hospital while poor Mum tried to staunch the flow of blood from one part of my anatomy or another.

I don't remember ever being able to sleep well as a child, and to this day I often have trouble falling into a deep sleep. In our house, we were all constantly alert in case Dad started shouting and storming about, as he so often did. Mum often had to spend much of the night in a sleeping bag on the floor at the side of my bed to calm me down. When I was asleep, she would tiptoe back to her own bed, only to find that, half an hour later, I would wake again and need her to come back and go through the routine all over again. Daniel also found it awfully difficult to sleep, and Mum would take him downstairs in the middle of the night so that I would not be disturbed. Daniel was awake most nights between two and five, and Mum would try to keep him entertained while she caught up with the family's ironing. When Daniel finally fell asleep again, Mum would creep back to bed beside Dad, hoping for a few hours' respite before another day started, with all the same challenges and setbacks as usual, and hoping that he would not stir, roll over, and demand that she do something for him.

Chapter Two: Happy Families

One day when I was seven, there was a heavy snowfall and all the schools closed early. Laboriously pushing Daniel through the snow in his buggy, Mum came to collect me and Jason from school and bring us home. We had moved house and now, instead of the small terraced house that I remember from my very early childhood, we were in a larger house on a quiet street with a back garden and a small, steep driveway to the front. It was a more middle-class area that, no doubt, reflected my father's feeling that he was entitled to a good standard of living because he was from a respectable family. I am sure that his parents had provided him with the down payment.

The snow was already about six inches deep when we arrived home, so you can imagine how excited Jason and I were at the prospect of having time off school to play outside. I had never seen anything so beautiful as that freshly fallen snow. I thought that I might go over to my little friend Elizabeth, who lived two doors down with her parents, Sheila and Dave, and her sister Rachel. I loved Elizabeth. She let me push her dolly in its pram, and I let her ride my bike and, if we were both really good, sometimes her mum would let us go down to the local chipper for a portion of chips to share between us.

"I can't believe it!" I said to Mum. "Look at this snow. Me and Elizabeth are going to make a snowman and throw snowballs!"

"I've got more good news for you, too," Mum said, with one of those rare smiles that lit up her face and turned her briefly back into the pretty girl who had originally attracted Dad's attention ten years before. "Your father is at home decorating your bedroom, and it is going to look fantastic! Aren't you lucky boys?"

Jason and I shared the huge front bedroom, and we had never seen it without the mould-flecked wallpaper hanging off the wall. I couldn't even imagine what the refurbished room must look like.

Jason and I raced upstairs to look at the new wallpaper. Mum was right; it *was* fantastic, even better than I imagined. They had bought Walt Disney patterned wallpaper with all our favourite characters: Donald Duck, Goofy, and Snow White.

"Wow, Dad!" I shouted excitedly. "This is amazing!"

I was already imagining how great it would be to lie in bed that evening, looking at all the images and making up stories to myself. I thought happily that I might even invite my friend Lee over to play. Lee, who lived next door, was my best friend in the world, an even better friend than Elizabeth. We had been pals since even before starting together in school at the age of four. I had already begun becoming too embarrassed about the state of our house to have Lee over, but now I would be delighted to show him my fancy new wallpaper.

Dad was red-faced and sweating and in a foul mood. He evidently had found it harder than he expected to hang the wallpaper. As soon as I saw the expression on his face as he turned around, I knew there would be trouble. We had all seen that expression before, more times than we could count. We should have crept away before something set him off, but we were so pleased about the new wallpaper that Jason and I just stood there in the doorway of our room, admiring it.

Dad didn't say anything, but he obviously found our enthusiasm insufferable.

"You two can just fuck off and give a man some bloody peace for once in your lives! I can't deal with the sight of you right now. Go to your mother and get out of my way."

"But Dad…"

I said *now!*"

Dad threw the wallpaper scraper across the room, and it struck Jason hard on the side of the head. Jason started to scream with the pain and shock as blood poured from the wound in his head. He put his hand up to feel the stream of blood and screamed even harder when he saw how much of it there was. I just stood there, feeling helpless and afraid. What if I was next? What should I do, or not do, to avoid attracting Dad's attention? Frozen to the spot, I just stood and stared. Dad looked thunderous. He started to approach Jason, the threat that there was more where that came from implicit in every motion.

"What the fuck have you done now, you stupid little git?" Dad asked Jason in a threatening manner. "What are you screaming about? I'll *give* you something to scream about if you are not careful."

Jason must have realised that he was in for more, too, because he stopped screaming as suddenly as he had started, and just held the side of his head and stared at Dad with big, wide eyes. Shocked out of my torpor, I took him by the hand and we rushed down the stairs to Mum, who was on her way to find out what all the commotion was about.

"Oh, my God," she said in shock. "What has he done now? Why does he always have to ruin everything?"

"He hit Jason in the head," I said. "He made him bleed."

"It was an accident," Jason added, half-choked by tears. His teeth were stained red with the blood that was running into his mouth. He didn't want to get in any more trouble than he was already in.

"Just get yourself down these bloody stairs!" Mum yelled at Dad. "You're taking us to the hospital. You've gone and done it this time!"

For once, confronted with the sight of blood pouring out of Jason's head, Mum had managed to assert herself. Dad put on his coat and went to start the car outside, muttering curses under his breath, but not putting up any resistance. Mum put my duffel coat on, and got Jason into his anorak and Daniel wrapped up. She fetched a cold compress for Jason's head. We all piled into the car, and Dad drove through the snow and ice to get us all to Oldham Hospital. He deposited us at the door and left.

"I don't suppose you'll be home to cook some dinner for me," he said to Mum as she got out of the car. "So I'm going out. Don't wait up."

The hospital was packed to the rafters with people who had fallen in the snow and had broken arms or legs or dislocated hips. Mum made her way through the crowd and registered Jason at the desk. Children always took priority, so Jason was going to be seen immediately.

The nurse in charge took one look at Jason, and then exchanged a meaningful glance with one of the doctors.

"We'll need to see your little boy on his own," she told Mum gently. "You can wait here, and we'll come and get you when we are ready for you."

I could see that Mum was scared. It was obvious that Jason had not suffered from an ordinary accident, and I imagine that she must have been petrified that the hospital staff thought her responsible for her child's injuries. She nodded mutely, and Jason was led away.

While we waited, Mum held my hand so tightly that it hurt. We both sat and watched Daniel sleeping in his buggy. A little bubble of snot expanded and contracted under his nostril as he breathed. After a while, my hand was so sore, I asked Mum to let me go, but she just clung to me even tighter.

"It's bad enough that Jason has been hurt," Mum said. "I can't have something happening to you as well. You're staying right here with me. I'll need you to help me if Daniel wakes up and starts to scream."

We were both frightened. The hospital was a strange, scary environment. The nurses wore starched uniforms, and everyone was in fear of the doctors. After what seemed like a long time, the doctor returned and called us into a side room where a woman was waiting to see Mum. I think she must have been some kind of social worker.

"I'm afraid you can't take the children home, Mrs Castree," the social worker told her with a matter-of-fact air. "Some concerns have been expressed about them, and you're all going to be transferred to spend the rest of the day in another part of the hospital."

I started crying.

"But there's nothing wrong with me!" I wailed. "I just want to go home!"

Mum didn't know what to do. She told me that everything would be all right, and that she would ring Nan, her mother, and ask her to come to the hospital to sort things out. Mum was about thirty at the time, but she seemed to be as much a frightened child as I was.

"Someone will sort it out," she said helplessly. "It's not my fault. I haven't done anything wrong."

As soon as Mum rang Nan, she came around to the hospital. First, she strode into Jason's room to make sure that he was all right. She demanded to see the doctors and hear their explanation. They told her that we had been detained because they were anxious about the number of times that Jason had been to the hospital with minor injuries. They were concerned that he was being abused at home. It turned out that the hospital suspected that Jason had been sexually as well as physically abused. He was given a thorough inspection, and our family was appointed a social worker who would look into our case and make recommendations on the basis of what she found.

While the adults talked, we boys were sent into the enclosed garden at the hospital to play. I know now that we were being watched to see how we related to one another. Eventually, Mum was told that we could leave the hospital, but that we should go to our grandmother's. If we were taken back home to Dad, they would arrange for someone to remove us from our family home and put us into care. Mum just listened and nodded, without saying anything. As always, she was completely passive. She seemed almost relieved that somebody had taken charge and was telling her what to do.

After a week or so at Nan's, we were brought back home. Much as she loved and wanted to protect her children, Mum just couldn't bring herself to stay away from Dad, and Nan's constant criticisms were hard to take. Nan had little respect for Mum and her choices, and whenever she complained about Dad or anything else, she just told her that she had made her bed, and now she had to lie in it.

After some time away, Mum might have thought that Dad would be remorseful about what he had done, and that things would get better. She was always hopeful that if only she did exactly what Dad told her, things would get better for us all.

***

When Dad cut loose, Mum would grab me and Daniel and run to Beryl and Tony next door.

Beryl would ring the police, who would come and give him a talking to. Once they put him in a cell overnight to cool off. A social worker called Doreen came to the house for a while. I can remember having to sit in a room listening to a tape about relaxation and family interaction that was supposed to help. After a while, Social Services determined that we were not at risk any more, that Dad was a sufficiently reformed character, and that was the last of Doreen. Although the beatings and the psychological abuse continued, we never saw a social worker again. Dad said that he was from a good family, and that his parents were well-connected people who had money and contacts in high places. In those circumstances, he said, it was absurd that he had had to deal with the indignity in the first place.

Looking back, I find it very difficult to understand why we were not taken into care. There was so much violence in our home, and Mum and we children – especially Jason, who usually fared the worst when Dad was in a bad mood – had been treated for so many injuries that it should have been painfully clear that this was a family dealing with horrendous domestic violence, and in need of serious intervention and help. Yet all Mum had to do to deflect attention from us was spend a few weeks at her mother's and the social workers backed off. At the time, I was absolutely terrified by the prospect of leaving Mum and going into care, but it couldn't have been worse than the reality of our lives with Dad.

After what had happened, you might have thought that Dad would be on his best behaviour from then on. He wasn't, and usually poor Jason was the one who took the brunt of his aggression. No matter how often Jason was beaten, he loved and looked up to Dad and just wanted his attention and approval.

When we were small, the constant shouts, violence and abuse that characterised Dad and Mum's relationship seemed normal, because it was all we knew. Growing older, we started to realise that the other children in our estate and in our classes at school didn't all come from homes where the plates were thrown at the walls, where Mum drank herself into oblivion to numb the pain, both physical and mental, and where Dad made little effort to hide some of his more unusual predilections from his children. We started to realise that we were different, and to feel as though we lived under some sort of dark cloud that did not cast its shadow on the other families we knew.

***

Some of my earliest memories are of Dad taking me kerb-crawling with him. He didn't actually have sex with the prostitutes in front of me, but he would stop the car and get their numbers to ring later on, and he left me in no doubt about what they were going to do when they got together. He would slap them on their PVC-clad bums as he turned away to get into the car and tell me that this one had "great tits" or that one had "a fantastic arse". This behaviour made me feel uncomfortable because it seemed odd, and because I had started to realise that it was not something that other people's dads did.

Later on, I often wondered why Dad had wanted to have a family at all. He clearly didn't like us – even hated us – and we could all see that he had no respect or love for Mum. The older I got, the more I understood about Dad's infidelities. The words "sex" and "whore" acquired meaning, and by the time I was reaching the end of junior school, I knew exactly what Dad was spending the housekeeping money on. Dad did nothing to hide it; in fact, he loved talking to us boys about his sexual habits and his other women. He seemed to get a kick out of seeing how he embarrassed us.

"If I can't get what I want," he would say, "I just go and get it elsewhere. Women are sluts and whores and they'll do whatever you want when you flash the cash. Anyway, marriage is just legalised prostitution. You'll understand why when you grow up. Women are good for one thing, and one thing only."

Dad felt that when they got married, he had bought Mum and that she belonged to him now and was supposed to submit to him in every possible way, including tolerating his many infidelities. Mum had had quite a good job as a young woman, working as a telephonist. If she'd stayed at work, she would have had a reasonable chance of advancement. But Dad had insisted that she give work up and stay at home to raise the children. He would have hated for her to have money of her own, as then he wouldn't have been able to control every aspect of her life the way he did. By ensuring that he was the only source of financial resources, Dad had Mum just where he wanted her. He had all the money, and he got to decide how much he gave her for housekeeping. He arranged for the child benefit to be lodged to his account. If there were extra expenses, or Mum ran out of money, she didn't get it, because the housekeeping money was supposed to last all week, and it was her fault if it didn't. As she would get slapped around when she asked for more, she became quite good at managing on very little, and we all got used to having cereal for our evening meal so that Dad could enjoy his beloved curries.

Dad was proud of being kinky, and was perfectly happy discussing it openly. He thought that it made him more interesting and in some way better and more important than ordinary men with more vanilla tastes in the bedroom. He liked to be tied up while being beaten by a woman dressed in schoolgirl costume, so he kept a washing line, porn videos, and canes for whipping in a wardrobe in their bedroom. At the weekends, I helped Mum tidy the house, which meant that I saw the schoolgirl costumes and the other paraphernalia Dad used.

"Sorry, Nick," Mum would say. "You know how he is. It's not worth making a fuss!"

I didn't have many friends, but I became reluctant to invite the few I had to our house in case they saw the things that I did and realised just how different our family was. While I felt sorry for Mum, because I could see how humiliated she felt, I could never understand why she was so open about Dad's sexual habits. Looking back, I can see that I was literally the only person Mum had to talk to at the time. She had no friends, her mother had told her she'd made her choice and had to stick with it, and she must have felt that she had literally no other option. Daniel was too young to talk to and Jason loved Dad, even though Dad treated him like shit. Mum turned me into her best friend and her carer and, seeing no other option, I accepted this role and did my best to fill it.

***

Despite the fact that he was no oil-painting with his balding head, his remaining hair pulled into a greasy ponytail at the back, Dad was good at singling out girls who might be interested in him, or at least prepared to pretend that they were. He looked for overweight girls who weren't the brightest and were insecure about their looks and their performance at school. Girls who lived in families even more dysfunctional than ours. Girls who had maybe had a child or two while they were still in their teens. Girls whose own fathers beat them up and told them they were ugly. Girls whose only hope of avoiding the dole queue was marrying a man who would be prepared to support them. Then, when he had identified them, he showered them with gifts and took them to hotels. He bought them booze and drugs. Before long, they were eating out of his hand. When we went to the market stall, we often found one perched on his knee, out of her head on drugs, giggling at his jokes and the fact that he was running his hands all over her.

Although I knew about kinky sex, and the fact that Dad liked to sleep with other women, on the matter of ordinary sex, I remained extremely ignorant. Our school was not very progressive when it came to sex education, and I think my only exposure to an ordinary discussion of the birds and the bees was the day we were shown an old-fashioned film about puberty on the overhead projector. Because I was curious about sex, occasionally I would take one of Dad's porn videos and watch it when he wasn't there. While I quickly learned about the mechanics of heterosexual sex, I remained none the wiser about what a normal, ordinary sex life was like.

***

We were not a religious family, but at Nan's insistence, we went to Sunday School at the local Church of England. I liked Sunday School because it provided us with a peaceful period of time away from all the shouting. I sat there enjoying the calm while the Bible stories went in one ear and out the other. Dad was prepared to put up with it because it was free, and because he wouldn't have to drive us anywhere – that was the reason why scouts or swimming were out of the question, not to mention the theatre workshop that I desperately wanted to do, and that the school had recommended for me. I would have loved to have a dog, but I couldn't because Daniel was allergic to dog fur. We were allowed to have some cats. One day, Daniel put one of the cats out as we were going to school and she never came back.

"You're a cat killer, aren't you?" Dad taunted Daniel from then on. Daniel would cry, because he had loved the cat, and Dad would laugh.

"If you loved her so much," he would say, "you wouldn't have let her out. She probably got squashed by a car and turned into a cat pancake."

***

We didn't do much together as a family, but we did occasionally watch TV. As always, Dad was in charge, so he was the one who got to decide what we looked at. He liked sci-fi, such as Star Wars and Star Trek, and half-heartedly followed some of the soaps, but he hated anything related to the news and would get really angry if anyone tried to watch Crimewatch UK, which was about the latest crimes, and unsolved crimes that the police were looking for help with.

"Who's watching that bloody muck?" he would say. "That's not why I pay the fucking television licence. Turn that shit off."

Leaving aside the fact that he left the TV licence unpaid, it made sense for Dad to prefer sci-fi to Crimewatch, because he lived for fantasy, in more ways than one. He made his living selling comic books and porn mags that sold diverse forms of fantasy to his customers. Sex for him involved imagining different scenarios, using props and costumes, and getting his rocks off on a story that he had invented himself, and he put a certain amount of effort into the fantasy that he was a normal family man with a happy wife and kids at home. The latter fantasy made it easier for him to pursue his real interest, which was persuading girls and vulnerable young women to do what he wanted, and to hang out with other middle-aged men who had similar interests to himself.

When I went into the shop at the weekend, I met these men, all of whom looked a lot like him – pasty faced from spending too much time indoors, balding, and greasy. They used to take the porn mags down off the shelf and pass them around, sniggering at the pictures of women and girls exposing their genitals for the world to see. They thought they were cool, but to a teenage boy it was just revolting, and whenever I found Dad with a young girl perched on his lap, I wondered what she saw in him.

At this time, Dad seemed to become a lot more stressed than usual and he began to drink more heavily. He also became more tolerant of Mum's drinking and prepared to extend the housekeeping money to accommodate it. When we all went to Tesco to do the weekly shop, he would buy bottles of whisky for him and brandy for her, and they would down a bottle a night until one or both of them passed out in the living room in front of the TV.

I had just started secondary school, and I was old enough to know that it was not safe to be around two alcoholics. The house could go on fire, and they would not even wake up. I wondered where Daniel and I could go if things got even worse. Jason was a young adult now, and involved in a relationship, but Daniel was still a small child, and I felt responsible for him. I knew we couldn't go to Nan's, because she hated us and considered us to be Mum's mistake. All the love she had in her heart was reserved for Jason, to whom she gave whatever he wanted. She gave him his first car, his motorbike, and money to take his girlfriend out, but Daniel and I were just a waste of space in her eyes. I was sure that if only I made a bigger effort, and made myself more loveable, Nan would learn to tolerate me. I drew her pictures, and spent my pocket money on little gifts for her, and found my offerings in the bin. Nan was also increasingly impatient with Mum, who was now drinking heavily, as well as failing at marriage and life in general.

"I wish my father was still here," Mum said. "I loved my dad."

Mum's father had died quite young. Apparently, he had been supportive of her as her mother never was.

Nan had no interest in hearing about it: "Even he would have told you to get off your backside and do something," she said. "What's wrong with you? Why can't you be more like your cousins?"

Mum's cousins all had jobs and nice houses and Mum had neither.

"You don't even stand up straight," Nan would continue. "Look at you. Why can't you hold your head up high, like your cousins do? You walk around the place looking like you have something to apologise for. I didn't raise you to do that. And don't get me started on your drinking. I can smell it on you. You're pathetic. No wonder the best man you were able to snag was that Ron. Well, it was your decision, and now you've got the rest of your life to regret it!"

Nan often compared Mum unfavourably to herself. She had gone straight back to work when Mum was born, and she had managed her husband's wages. He had earned fairly good money as a long-distance lorry driver, and he had meekly handed the money over to her at the end of every week. Nan was used to being in charge, and she could not understand why her daughter was so weak. Although she was comfortably off, she never gave her any money, saying that she would just spend it on drink, or that it would end up in Dad's pocket.

Nan despised Mum for not building a better life for herself, and not standing up for herself and her needs, but Mum had been beaten into submission by this stage, both literally and figuratively. Dad had broken her nose and left her bruised from head to toe more times than I can count. She had often ended up in hospital, but she just kept going back because she had nowhere else to go and didn't have enough self-respect to attempt to carve out a new life for herself without him. Now that they were both drinking so heavily, the domestic abuse was even worse. They got into drunken fights, and he would throw her down the stairs, and then tear everything off the walls and throw it down after her. I was so worried about Mum that I started mitching off school to keep the house clean (getting away from the bullies was just a bonus), reasoning that if Dad had fewer things to complain about, Mum was less likely to get beaten up. Cleaning the house gave me a sense of being in control, too.

Chapter Three: The Jumped-up Fairy

I had realised that I was a bit different to the other boys I knew from the age of eight or so. That was also around the time when people had started calling me names because they thought I was a bit effeminate and "soft" and they were all primed by a macho culture and children's comics like the Beano to feel that bullying "softies" was the right thing to do and that they had a licence to do so. This feeling of difference grew as I did, and so did the name-calling and bullying.

"Come here, you little poof," Dad used to say. "Or I'll bloody well give you something to cry about. Stop mincing about like that. Why can't you walk like a proper boy? What the hell is wrong with you?"

"Look at your brother," Dad would say to Jason in disgust, if he didn't like the way I moved across the room, or if I did something that annoyed him. "He's nothing but a jumped-up fairy. A fucking hysterical queen."

I should clarify that Dad disliking me because he considered me to be a "fairy" meant that I was added to a long list of people he disliked because of who they were, or who he considered them to be. Dad hated the Asians he saw down the market ("Pakis"). He hated black people ("dirty fucking niggers"). He despised women who did not fit the narrow criteria that he considered acceptable for feminine behaviour ("frigid bitches," "cunts," "fucking slags"). Dad was very good at hating people; it was one of his specialties, and he engaged in it all the time. His own parents were from an older generation, and were quite conservative, but I never heard them using hateful language or witnessed them disrespecting someone simply because of who they were, so I can't blame them for this aspect of Dad's behaviour; it was all him.

Because I was used to Dad being hateful, I could cope with his behaviour, but it really hurt me when Jason joined in, because we had been very close when we were younger, and I still loved him very much. We had always fought and squabbled, but Jason was my big brother, and I looked up to and admired him. I think that he was fond of me too, until Dad's poison, and Jason's burning need to be loved, or at least liked, by Dad promoted him to call me horrible names. He never apologised, but sometimes when Dad wasn't around I caught him looking at me like maybe he wanted to.

Whatever it was that Dad had picked up about me, it was also evident to the other kids in school. As we had all grown older, the fact that I was badly dressed compared to most of them was increasingly apparent, and my "effeminate" appearance just added fuel to the fire. The school was extremely passive in the face of any bullying behaviour, and I had nobody to turn to there. Already a quiet, introverted child, I never tried to stand up for myself.

***

By now, Jason was getting big and strong, and sometimes he and Dad got into fights at home, knocking each other around. Dad would follow Jason up to his room and get him up against the wall. Sometimes Mum would try to get between them, to stop Jason from getting hurt.

"He's just a boy, Ron!" she would plead. "Leave him alone. You're going to hurt him, and he shouldn't be encouraged to act out like this."

"Yeah, you *would* stand up for him, wouldn't you?" Dad would pant. "Kid needs some sense knocked into him. Get out of the fucking way, if you know what's good for you."

Afterwards, nursing his bruises, Jason would be remorseful for standing up to Dad. All he ever wanted was for Dad to love and respect him, and even the fistfights were Jason's attempt to impress Dad with how he was turning into a real man. Poor Jason kept on trying to get Dad to love him. As well as following his lead in tormenting me, he bought him gifts and cards. He always gave him a card on Father's Day, but Dad threw it in the bin. When Jason, hurt, asked Mum why, she just shrugged and said she didn't know.

"It's just the way he is," she said. "Try not to let it bother you too much."

When Jason figured out that one of the ways to get on Dad's good side was by bullying me and calling me horrible names, he had a tool to use in his quest to be loved, and he used it every chance he got.

As I got older, my relationship with Dad and Jason continued to deteriorate, and as I headed into my teens, I became increasingly aware of, and concerned about, my sexuality, wondering if Dad and Jason were right, and I was a "faggot" and a "fairy". By the time I was thirteen or so, I gave up on trying to get back into Jason's good books and went my own way, wondering how I would ever accept myself as I was.

***

Because Dad's porn videos were all over the house, they were a ready source of sex education for Jason and me. Being a few years older, and a good-looking lad, Jason didn't find it hard to attract girls. By the time he was in his late teens, he had a lovely girlfriend, a pretty girl from an educated family. While I never had friends to the house because I had become so embarrassed by the condition of our home, and by Dad's behaviour, Jason was so anxious to impress Dad and gain his respect that he brought his girlfriend home. Predictably, Dad leered at her, and then gave Jason pornography for him and his girlfriend to watch together.

"So you can see how it's done!" Dad laughed. "Ha ha, got to treat a girl right, eh?"

Predictably enough, Jason's relationship broke up not long after that.

***

As I approached my teens, my hormones raged and, like any adolescent, I became interested in sex. While I had begun to understand that I was attracted to boys, I didn't know anything about gay relationships, and most of what I knew about sex was gleaned from lying in bed with my head under the pillow trying not to listen to Dad raping Mum in the room next door ("Get off me, Ron, get off. Please, get off.") or from Dad's ribald comments about women to his friends. Back in the early 90s, there were very few positive depictions of homosexuals on TV or in the print media, and most of the time when homosexuality was mentioned it was in the context of discussing the AIDS epidemic and how many people had died since AIDS was first identified in the early 1980s, and it all sounded quite frightening. I tried not to think about the sexual feelings that often threatened to overwhelm me, because I associated physical attraction with Dad's behaviour, which I increasingly realised was not just inappropriate, but off the charts, and because Dad and Jason had made it very clear that they thought I was disgusting, because I was a bit different.

***

If we were driving around our local area as a family, Dad loved to humiliate Mum by openly admiring the women and girls he saw on the street.

"Phwoar, look at the tits on that," he would say as a thirteen-year-old girl walked by in her school uniform. "Look at that, Jason. You won't be interested, Nick. You're a bit of an arse bandit, aren't you?"

"For God's sake, Ron," Mum would hiss. "She's only a young girl. Don't do this in front of the boys. This is inappropriate."

"Maybe I wouldn't, if *you* gave me something to look at," Dad would retort. "If you took better care of yourself, I might be less inclined to notice. The way things are, you can't be surprised I have a bit of a wandering eye."

"You're embarrassing me!"

"I don't give a shit."

Sometimes the girls that Dad admired so openly were even younger; primary school girls with their hair in ponytails, who didn't even need a wear a bra yet.

"I'd give her one," Dad would say, tapping his fingers on the steering wheel. "Give her one until she begged me to stop."

"She's a child!" Mum would say. "You're disgusting. I can't believe you think it's all right to talk like that in front of the boys. What kind of an example are you setting for them?"

"What's disgusting is a wife who lets herself go to seed! What's disgusting is a mother who lets her son grow up to be a fucking poofter and doesn't do anything to stop it. If I have anything to do with it, I won't let *my* sons grow up to be pussy-whipped."

We boys reacted as best we could in the back seat, pretending that we couldn't hear him, or staring fixedly at our laps and hoping that none of our classmates would notice us with the dirty old man in the driver's seat.

Sometimes Dad would turn to us and address us directly.

"Boys," he would say. "Take it from me; when you get older, you need to find yourselves women – OK, Nick, probably not you, you're a nancy-boy – who will give you what you need. I've had plenty of them, and I've videoed what a real man gets up to, so if you want to know what that looks like, you only need to ask. There are plenty of tapes to go around, OK?"

Afterwards, Mum explained that Dad was very demanding, and that when she didn't please him, he felt that he had the right to look outside their marriage. We just took this at face value, not realising that being told about our father's sex life so graphically was abusive in itself. Nobody ever told us what abuse was, how to recognise it, and what to do if we were ever victims of it. There was no program at school to inform us, and we simply didn't know what sex abuse was. If we had known, we might have been able to recognise that the teenage girls Dad used to lure into the shops with money and other gifts – the chubby, plain, awkward girls with terrible home lives and low self-esteem, the girls who featured on those home-made porn videos he talked about, sucking him off or letting him beat them – were his victims just as much as we were.

***

Dad and Mum had both been drinking heavily since my early childhood, but now Dad's back was acting up and booze was no longer enough to help him deal with the pain. He got some pills from the doctor, but he still wanted more. One day, I came home from school and found Dad burning something on a spoon over the gas hob in the kitchen. Because there was a big drug problem in the wider area, and we had been given talks at school on how important it was to avoid drugs, with dire warnings about how easy it was to become addicted, I knew straight away what he was doing. I stood and stared, genuinely shocked for once. I had seen Dad getting up to all sorts of things, but this one was new, and I wasn't sure how I was supposed to react.

"What the fuck do you think you are looking at, you fucking queer?" Dad shouted. "It's none of your fucking business but, for your information, this is for my bad back. I've only done it in providing for my ungrateful fucking family."

"Get out of here, Nick," Mum said. "It's OK. Go and do your homework. It's for his back. He'll feel better in a few minutes."

I left the room. I could see from the expression in Mum's eyes that if I said anything to annoy him, she would end up paying the price for it. I didn't want that on my conscience. Dad spent the rest of the evening cradling a bottle of whisky in front of the television as though it was his child. Between the various prescription medications that the doctor had prescribed for his pain, the booze, and the illegal hard drugs, Dad was like a powder-keg waiting to go off.

***

Because my family life and our home were such a mess, it was a great comfort to me to keep my bedroom tidy. A tidy room provided me with a little oasis of calm and a sense of being in control that I found tremendously rewarding. No matter how shit things were for me at school and at home, there was at least one place where everything was where it was supposed to be. At first, to achieve the sense of order that I longed for, all I needed to do was keep my room in order, but as time passed, I started to develop rituals that helped me to feel better about things. If I folded my clothes and put them away, I would have to open the wardrobe door to look inside and make sure that everything was in order over and over again. I often made my bed five or six times to get it just right. I cleaned the tatty carpet on the floor several times a day. I loved the fact that my room was perfect, unlike the rest of the house, even though my obsessive rituals took up more and more of my time and sometimes stopped me from doing my homework. Downstairs, the dining room was piled high with Dad's comics, books, and dirty magazines, as he used the house to store the publications he sold at work. In both the dining and the living room, the wallpaper was peeling off because it was damp, and because one of the cats had taken to scurrying up the wall and scratching it off until it hung down in long, tatty ribbons. There was mould in the corners of the rooms because nobody ever opened a window to air the house.

I had started feeling embarrassed about letting friends see the inside of my house a few years before, but now I realised that it was out of the question, because nobody else had a house as filthy and disgusting as ours, and nobody else had a father who left his home-made porn lying about for all to see.

Lee from next door and I were still close, but I told him that I didn't want him coming to my house anymore. Because Lee knew what our home was like, he understood my reticence and didn't say anything.

I still went to Lee's house, which was absolutely perfect. The carpets were vacuumed, the tiles in the kitchen and bathroom gleamed, and his mum kept fresh flowers in the living room and baked home-made biscuits for us to nibble after school. Lee's dad was working on the oil rigs in Dubai and his parents were doing well financially, so they sold their house and moved to a fancier area. Our friendship continued, and Lee's mum, Tricia, used to come over to ours in their car, pick me up, and bring me to their place so that I could hang out with Lee and eat with their family. I thought that Tricia was amazing. She talked to me as though she was really interested in what I had to say, remembered what I liked to eat, and was always happy to welcome me into their beautiful home. I realised that not all mums were like mine – lost, drunk, and self-absorbed – and that there were many who were happy in their marriages, had kind husbands who loved them, and who found fulfilment in caring for their families and providing for them. I had always loved Lee's family, but now I fantasised that his mum and dad were my parents, and I imagined how different my life would be if they were. I imagined having parents who showed some affection and told me that they cared about me and my feelings. As it was, Tricia was my guardian angel. If I looked hungry, she made sure that I had something nutritious to eat. If things were really bad at home, she let me stay the night. She even tried to help Mum, on those rare occasions when Mum went over to her house for a cup of tea and a chat.

"Just leave him, Bev," she would say. "It would be better for you and the kids. Nobody should have to put up with the things you do. You deserve more."

"How would I manage?" Mum would sigh. "I don't have work. I don't have any money. I've lost my looks and nobody else would want me."

"It will be tough at the beginning, but you're still young; you can start over again. The council will help with a flat and you can get a job and start standing on your own two feet before you know it. And it's not true that you've lost your looks. You just need to start feeling more confident and take care of yourself better. You really don't have to go on like this. You've got a choice."

"You're right, Tricia," Mum would agree. But she never did anything about it.

I was no longer as close to my neighbour Elizabeth as I had been when we were little. She was soaring through adolescence. She was beautiful and talented, and already training to be an opera singer, which meant that she went on a lot of trips. However, her parents had already provided me with another example of what a mutually respectful and loving couple looked like, and they were still kind and polite when we met – though they were understandably wary of Dad, who was a loose cannon. Elizabeth's dad, Dave, was a good runner, and I used to see him training in the neighbourhood. He would smile and wave and sometimes stop for a brief chat.

Looking back now, I can see that various adults in the area were watching out for me the whole time, and making my life less awful than it could have been. Elizabeth's family had got their kittens from the same neighbour who had given us ours, which meant that they had an excuse to stop for a chat. We could talk about the cats and what they were up to, while they subtly checked me for obvious bruises and harm. They invited me into their homes when they "just happened" to have made more for dinner than they needed, and in that way ensured that I had at least the occasional proper meal. They did all of this despite knowing how dangerous Dad was, and for this I will always be more grateful than they could ever imagine. Above all, however, by showing me what real, happy families looked like, they gave me a morsel of hope for the future and the sense that, one day, perhaps my life would be different.

***

At school I was struggling badly, both socially and academically. There was no chance of getting any help with my homework from Mum and Dad, and I was so shy I never asked for anything. Almost everyone, including me, seemed to accept that I just wasn't the brightest and was simply putting in time until I was old enough to leave and pick up some menial work. Some of the rougher kids had picked up on the fact that I was a bit "softer", a bit more "girly" than other lads, and tormented me with the same ugly words that Dad used to describe me. A jumped-up fairy. A faggot. An arse-bandit. They made vulgar jokes about what they assumed to be my sexual preferences. A couple of the teachers saw that I was vulnerable but, in the absence of a formal structure to help kids in my situation, there didn't seem to be much they could do. Two of the female teachers occasionally gave me a lift home or let me stay back after class to help out. This relieved some of the bullying, and possibly they were trying to give me the opportunity to speak out about what was going on, but I never did.

One of the few positive relationships I had at this time was with Sean, my mother's cousin's child. Trish was a single mum, because Sean's dad had been a waste of space, and had lost all interest in his child as soon as he realised that he had cerebral palsy and was going to be difficult to care for. The whole situation was really tough for Trish, and she often came around to Nan's to get a break from being on her own with a severely disabled child. Trish drank tea and talked to Nan about how difficult and stressful her life was, and I played with Sean and tried to interact with him. Sean was badly disabled, but also very bright, and I could see how frustrating his life was. He spent most of his time strapped into a buggy and couldn't even walk or talk. Only his alert expression showed that he was taking in everything he saw in the world around him and thinking about it. When they visited, I took Sean out of his buggy and held him up so that he could get a little exercise. I talked to him and tried to understand his attempts to communicate. I think that I empathised with Sean because I thought that I understood how he felt, tied into a situation he had no control over, and unable to express himself.

**

I began to toy with the idea of simply not existing any more. Of going to sleep and not waking up in the morning to find out that everything was still shit. Of not having to deal with any of the pain, misery, and torment that seemed to be my natural portion in life. I wasn't brave enough to actively contemplate suicide, but I thought that if I worked my way up to it, one day I might be, and then all my problems would be over, forever. I practiced jumping down the last four or five steps of our stairs, imagining that one day I would throw myself down from the top and whack my head off the radiator, and that then it would all be over for good. If it hadn't been for the fact that I knew from my friends' parents that life was not always as awful as it was in our home, I think I would have done much worse.

Chapter Four: First Times

I drifted badly in secondary school, which I attended in our local area along with the same kids I had been in primary school with. The only reason why I didn't get into trouble all the time was the fact that I was so quiet. Rather than causing problems, I just sat at the back of the classroom and let it all wash over me. I didn't attract a lot of attention from the teachers, and the fact that I was falling behind in almost every subject was mostly overlooked. The only thing that I could really engage with was my obsessive cleaning, and my firm conviction that I could only feel OK if everything around me, and in my life, was in order. Unfortunately, my obsessive compulsions also made it harder for me to engage with other young people and make friends, and they consumed most of the intellectual and emotional energy that I might otherwise have used on schoolwork and study.

Every so often, one of the more perceptive teachers, who had noticed that I was lost and alone at the bottom of the classroom, drew me aside for a "little chat."

"Look, Nick," they would say, "I think you're capable of a lot more than you are managing to achieve. I get the sense that you're quite a bright lad, really. You just need to apply yourself more. You'd be able to stay on and get your A-levels, and then you would have so many more options in life. Just a few more years and a little bit of effort, and think of all you could do. Go to college, get a good job... you know, it is so much easier to get a mortgage if you have a college education. You want to get on in life, don't you?"

Despite the mildly supportive comments of a few teachers, I didn't like school, and felt quite sure that education did not have anything for me. While I did have a few friends, most of the time I felt very alone, and when I wasn't alone I was being bullied for wearing the wrong clothes or being too effeminate, or both. The bullies were typically not the highest academic achievers, but they had considerable intelligence and ingenuity when it came to devising new ways to make my life utterly miserable. There was no formal structure in place in school to protect the kids like me, who stood out because they wore ugly, scruffy clothes with the wrong labels on, or because they were gay, or both, and were treated badly.

I remember Mrs Brooks, the science teacher, encouraging me to stay on in the lab after science class to do my homework and her steady, quiet presence while she tidied up the Bunsen burners as I sat with my books, my eyes glazed over rather than focused on the words they contained. I can see now that she was trying to be kind, to keep me safe. Mrs Brooks tried to encourage me to go to college too, but when I imagined yet more years in the classroom, all I could envision was more bullying and torture, and I wanted none of it.

***

While all of this was going on, I was increasingly aware of my sexuality. Until now, I hadn't completely understood what Dad and Jason meant when they called me a "poof" and "fairy", although I did have a sense of myself as different to other boys. Now I understood it perfectly and graphically. It meant that the lips I wanted to kiss were other boys', and that the bodies I found attractive and wanted to touch were slim boys' bodies like my own. While I found it easier to talk to girls, they did not arouse any sexual interest in me; their curves and lipstick and made-up faces did not excite me in any way, and I preferred a man's low voice to a woman's higher tones. When I closed my eyes, and fantasised about the future, I imagined a Prince Charming rather than a Snow White or a Belle, and in those fantasies, *I* was the one swept off his feet, cared for, protected, and loved. I was the one who allowed himself to be wooed by a handsome suitor, and I was the one who might one day consent to give his hand in marriage.

This understanding was a breakthrough for me, but it was not one that I welcomed, even though it just felt right in so many ways. I knew that if I told Mum, she would tell Dad, and then he would get angry and beat me up. I knew that if the other kids in school found out, then they would make fun of me and beat me up. I knew that if I told the teachers, they would advise me to keep it to myself, or maybe suggest that I have a chat with the GP. I understood very well that this was something that I needed to take care of myself. For now, I kept my fantasies of falling in love and feeling someone's strong arms around me to myself. On the other hand, I started to dress and move in a way that I would now refer to as "camp", although I didn't know that word at the time. Dad found it extremely annoying ("you're embarrassing me in that get-up, you fucking queer") and showered me with insults when I was working for him in the shop, but being able to manage an aspect of my identity in that way gave me a sense of being in control of at least one small corner of my life.

***

When Stefan Kiszko was released from jail in 1992, everyone was talking about it. Lesley Molseed's murder was of the few high-profile cases that had ever taken place in the area, and the local people knew Stefan's parents, or at least knew who they were. Stefan's photo had been plastered all over the papers when he was put in jail, and now it was plastered all over them again. Many of the locals vividly remembered when Lesley had gone missing, and the devastating news that she had been found dead. People had found some relief in the idea that at least the killer had been found and sent to prison, but now they knew that it had been the wrong man all along. We had all been told as children to be careful of talking to strange men, and related the tale of Stefan Kiszko, the big, fat man who had stolen Lesley Molseed and killed her. Now it turned out that the story had never been true.

The Kiszkos were part of a small Ukrainian community that had moved to England after the war to work in cotton mills, and had settled in the Rochdale area. They couldn't go back to Ukraine because the iron curtain had closed all around the Soviet countries, and they never really fitted in in the UK because they were different, they had strange names and accents, and they tended to keep themselves to themselves. Stefan was doubly different because he was very overweight, he looked odd, and his childlike manner disturbed some people. Although he had a civil service job, he stayed at home with his widowed mother, Charlotte, and only smiled absently when the local children shouted names after him and threw things. He did not seem to quite belong in this world, and he annoyed people with his peculiar hobby of writing down car registration numbers. When three girls claimed that he had exposed himself to them a couple of days before the murder, that he would be convicted was pretty much a done deal. For a lot of people, it seemed to confirm the widely-held idea that anyone a bit different, and foreign on top of it, was automatically suspicious.

After Stefan was put in jail, his mother Charlotte started to campaign for his release, insisting that he was incapable of carrying out such a terrible crime. At first people ostracised her, horrified that she could stand up for her son, who had been convicted as a paedophile and a murderer. But she was persistent and, little by little, she managed to rally some of the community around her and convince them that Stefan could never have done what he had been accused of. Mrs Kiszko contacted Cyril Smith, the famous politician and my grandparents' friend, and asked him for help, but none was forthcoming. She had continued campaigning all through the 1980s, and occasionally the local newspapers had mentioned her efforts. Now it was all coming out. People had been very quick to assume that Stefan was guilty just because he looked odd, and because his family were foreigners who spoke with a strange accent. He had not been defended properly, the police had sewn him up, and the defending lawyer had not even presented the relevant evidence. The three girls who had identified him as exposing himself to them on the day of the murder admitted that they had made up the fake evidence for a laugh because they thought it was funny. Crimewatch UK ran a special episode about Stefan, with an overweight actor playing the man who had suffered in prison for so many years for a crime that he had not committed. Although Dad hated Crimewatch and didn't let us watch it when he was in the house, he was out that evening, and I turned it on, along with everyone else in the neighbourhood.

I have to admit, I found it quite exciting to think of something so high-profile happening in my home area. I didn't know the Kiszkos but I was aware of them, and of course everyone was talking about the case once Stefan was eventually cleared and released from jail. Mum's cousin Christine lived on the same housing estate as Charlotte Kiszko, I knew that Dad was from the area and had worked as a taxi driver there, and of course we had all been warned on multiple occasions to stay away from strange men, with the spectre of Stefan Kiszko raised as the demon who would scare us away from doing anything foolish.

"Hey Dad," I asked excitedly when he got home half way through the show. "Do you remember Stefan Kiszko? Did you ever meet him?"

I thought that Dad might have taken the Kiszkos as a fare at some point and might have an interesting story to tell that I could take to school and share with my classmates.

"No," said Dad. "And turn that crap off. You know I don't watch Crimewatch or any of that fucking shit."

Dad left the room in a huff and I kept watching. It emerged that the unfortunate Stefan Kiszko, who had by now served sixteen years of his sentence, could not have been guilty of killing Lesley Molseed. Lesley's killer had ejaculated on her, and Stefan had a medical condition that meant that he was incapable of producing sperm. This meant that Lesley's real killer was still at large and quite possibly living somewhere local, and suggested that someone in authority had been so anxious for Stefan to go to prison for the crime that they had been prepared to overlook the fact that he simply could not have been guilty of it.

Everyone was talking about Stefan Kiszko. I was in secondary school at that time, and the teenagers were all gossiping about it; the fact that the crime had a sexual element made it that much more interesting. Later that week, down at the shop, I heard Dad and his friends all joking about Stefan Kiszko, especially the fact that he should never have been convicted because he was incapable of producing sperm and Lesley Molseed's body had had her killer's sperm on it: "At least the murderer had some fucking balls," they sniggered. Dad laughed, but he changed the subject.

The same year as Stefan Kiszko's release, Dad joined a local gun club and bought guns. He became paranoid, leaping to his feet when he heard a car outside on the street, and lurking behind the net curtains with a gun. Although we were allowed to have pet cats, Dad shot at the neighbours' cats when he saw them parading around on our garden fence. He had trouble sleeping and kept a gun under the pillow, leaping up to point it out the window every time he thought he heard something strange. He started to talk in his sleep and would wake Mum up, mumbling, "I'm sorry, I'm sorry," or "They're coming to get me." Mum didn't ask him what his dreams were about, because she had already learned that asking too many questions often ended up with her being given a beating and a black eye. It was easier just to leave it.

Dad bought a gun safe for the house, where he kept his new toys – a couple of handguns, an air rifle with a long barrel, blue earmuffs, and tape. Sometimes he went down to the club, but mostly he played with his guns at home. Every day, he cleaned them and checked the sights by pointing them out the window.

"If you're not good, I might just shoot you one day," he said. "So you'd better watch out."

He laughed as though he had just said something hilarious, and we joined in so as not to annoy him, but none of us found it funny at all. Sometimes Dad got drunk and ran around the house with his guns, while we fled in terror. When he sobered up, he passed it off as a joke, but none of us were laughing.

Dad always kept his guns at the ready in case someone came to "get him". He said that he needed to be prepared to defend himself at any given moment.

"Who would want to get you, Dad?" I asked.

"Shut the fuck up and mind your own bloody business," he retorted.

We lived on a quiet street, and could hear every car that turned into it. Dad would be up at the curtains with his gun, ready to shoot at the slightest sound. Every time a car approached he seemed to panic, as though the person driving it was coming to get him. He was having trouble sleeping, and kept a gun near the bed in case someone came for him in the night. Mum contacted the police about his behaviour, and one of the officers came around for a chat, but apparently Dad had done nothing wrong and they couldn't take his guns away.

Mum tried to reason with Dad when he was being especially paranoid.

"Who do you *think* is coming for you, Ron?" she would say. "There's nobody there. Nobody is even giving you a second thought. They're all at home watching *Corrie* or eating their tea. People are just too busy to worry about what a comic book shop owner is up to after work."

"Oh, just leave it, Bev, just leave it," Dad would snap back. "You're like a dog with a fucking bone. Shut the fuck up."

***

Stefan Kiszko died of a heart attack, eighteen months after his release. His mother Charlotte died not long after that. They had not received the compensation they were entitled to, and the girls who had made false testimony against him had not apologised. There was another flurry of interest in the media because of the sheer poignancy of the situation, and then the story of Lesley Molseed became just another cold case that seemed like it would never be solved.

***

When I was fourteen, Grandad announced that he was going to take me to London on a trip to see all the sights. He had taken Jason a few years earlier, and now it was my turn. Grandma had died of cancer of the oesophagus a few years before, so he was alone now, and everyone agreed that it was good to see him getting out and about and taking an interest in things despite getting on in years. He still talked about his connection to Cyril Smith, the MP, and the garden parties that he and Grandma had attended with him back in the glory days. Every so often, he took out the condolence note that Cyril had sent him when Grandma died. It was written on a piece of paper with a Westminster heading, and Grandad was quite proud of it.

"Look at this, son," he would say. "That Cyril Smith is a good 'un. He doesn't forget who his real friends are."

I was so excited about going to the big city. I spent several days planning my outfit for the trip. Grandad and I went up on the train and stayed in a real hotel near London Bridge. Grandad took me to see Buckingham Palace and all the royal sights, explaining how Britain had once been at the head of a great empire, and that London was full of history.

"When you stand here and look at all of this," he said expansively, "you can feel proud about being a part of it."

We were on Westminster Bridge when I saw a boy who really got my heart racing. I blushed when I realised that Grandad had noticed the effect he had on me. He winked at me, but he didn't say anything.

After dinner that evening, I excused myself and went up to our hotel room, leaving Grandad sitting over a G&T in the hotel bar. I sat on the edge of my single bed and thought about the boy I had seen earlier, imagining how amazing it would be to be noticed and desired by someone like him. Would he want to kiss me? Would he let me kiss him? I became aroused, opened my shorts, and started to masturbate. I was so caught up in what I was doing, I didn't even notice when the door opened.

"Well, well," said Grandad. "What have we here?"

I jumped up guiltily, but he smiled at me reassuringly.

"Don't worry, Nick," he said. "You are a healthy young man and this is perfectly natural behaviour. You are not doing anything wrong, and don't let anyone tell you otherwise, all right?"

Then he reached out his hand and fondled me until, in a fog of confusion, I reached climax.

Grandad took a handkerchief out of his pocket and wiped his hand.

"We don't have to tell anyone about this," he said. "It is just our little secret. You don't want anyone to know what you've been up to, do you?"

I felt sick. I waited for Grandad to go to sleep and then I went into the bathroom and took a shower so long and so hot that my skin hurt all over.

We went home the next day, and I didn't tell anyone about what had happened. Mum said that it was nice to see me getting along so well with Grandad, and encouraged me to go up to his house several times a week.

"Go on, Nick," she said. "He's an old man and he's missed Grandma since she passed away. The company will do him good."

Grandad had moved into a retirement bungalow, as the old house was too big for an old man to take care of on his own and he wanted to free up some equity by selling it. The abuse continued and, after each episode, he gave me some money and reminded me that what we had just done was a secret. These encounters made me feel sick and guilty, but I thought that it was all my fault for being attracted to boys, and that there was nothing I could do to make it stop. I felt that in some way I was receiving a punishment that I deserved. I was sure that I would get in terrible trouble if anybody found out.

On some level, I had always known that Grandad liked boys. Clearly, he liked me. It all became a shameful problem for the family when Grandad molested a boy, in a local public toilet that was well-known for cruising, and was caught in the act by a police officer who had been casing the area because of its reputation. The lad was about my age, a good-looking boy who lived in foster care and went to my school. The local papers had a field day with the story, and I stayed away from school for a few days until the fuss died down. The police came around to our house to take a statement, and I told them and Mum that Grandad had molested me too.

"Why didn't you tell us, love?" Mum asked. "You never said. We didn't know."

I just stared at her. She was never available to talk to. When would I have told her? And what would she have done? She had never done anything about Dad's treatment of me, so why would I expect her to do something about Grandad's?

At school, I was so ashamed of Grandad and of myself that I shrank even more into my own shell. I didn't discuss the abuse or Grandad's legal case with anyone. Of course, all the kids knew about it, and I was the target of a great deal of teasing and bullying ("Hear your Grandad is a faggot and a paedo; do you turn him on?") that the teachers were either unaware of or didn't care about. I kept my eye on the clock, just waiting for three o'clock to arrive. My English teacher gave me a lift home occasionally, which provided some relief from the bullying. I remember leaning against the cool window in her car and wishing that she would take me back to her house – or anywhere, really, other than home. I imagined what it would be like sitting around the kitchen table with her and her family, having dinner and talking about what my day at school had been like, and then watching telly or going up to bed, knowing that I wouldn't have to listen to the shouting or Mum crying out because Dad was raping her yet again.

Grandad went to court, but he avoided a jail sentence because he was an old man in poor health and there was a suggestion that, in his seventies, he was not in full command of his faculties. The assault had been interrupted by the policeman before the boy had been badly hurt. The boy Grandad had assaulted returned to school, and although we knew each other to see, we never talked to each other or discussed what had happened. He may have guessed that I had experienced similar treatment to him, or perhaps he assumed that I was like my grandfather.

"Well," said Dad. "*I'm* not fucking taking care of him after that. Showing us all up like that. We're a laughing stock in the community."

Grandad was too frail to prepare his own meals, and Dad said that Mum had to do it because otherwise he wouldn't eat and would get sick and be even more of a burden. Because everyone felt that Grandad and I were close, I was roped in to help, and was often sent to his house at the weekends to help him out with chores and prepare his meals. Grandad still slipped me extra pocket money, but it didn't come without a price, and his abuse of me continued. My feelings were mixed. On the one hand, I knew that what he was doing to me was wrong, and I felt dirty and disgusting with each and every episode, but on the other, I was hoarding the money he gave me as a fund to use when I eventually worked up the courage to run away from home. I hated the abuse, but I didn't want my only source of money at the time to dry up. My plan was to wait until I had enough money, and then run away from home. I had no idea where I would go, or how I would manage to support myself, but I felt confident that I would work something out, and that it would be better than this.

Everyone in my family was an expert in knowing all about the secrets that should never be discussed. Somehow, while there were many matters that we never overtly discussed, on some level we were aware of many of the undercurrents in our lives.

When I found Grandad dead and naked about a year and a half after he had started abusing me, I understood straight away that he must have died with his lover Steven, a much younger man from the area whom he had been seeing for a number of years. Grandad had a bit of money from downsizing after his wife's death, and this was probably the main attraction, from Steven's point of view. Grandad was happy to spend money on Steven if that was what it took to keep him on board. Steven was often there when I called to the bungalow, and he usually made an excuse and left. I presume that he and Grandad had been having sex when Grandad had a heart attack and died. At least he went with a smile.

Grandad, an abuser, and a gay man who had never formally come out of the closet, was my first role model of a gay man, but he was not the only one. Grandma's brother Ronnie was gay, and everyone knew it. Uncle Ronnie was tall, slim, elegant, and well-to-do. Uncle Ronnie was someone in my family I could look up to. While he was not deeply involved with us, we saw him from time to time at family occasions. Even in old age, he was tall, elegant, and well-spoken and, while I did not realise it at the time, did provide me with an example of how a well-adjusted, happy gay man could be. I think that Grandad envied his courage in being an overtly gay man at a time when most gay men did their best to get married to women so that they could pass under the radar. After all, being gay was illegal in those days and men could be, and often were, prosecuted and thrown in jail for having consensual sex, or a loving relationship with another man. Grandad had been an army man before he got married, and I am sure that he experienced plenty of "action" when he was with the forces. When he came home, he had narrowed in on Grandma, who was attractive, respectable, and well-to-do. As Grandad was from a roughish working-class background, he landed on his feet with her; she was a one-way ticket to the middle classes. After having one child with him, she was prepared to sleep in separate rooms and pretend that none of his multiple gay relationships were happening. I have often wondered if Ronnie was the one whom Grandad really loved.

Grandma had been descended from a genteel family that had started out in service to an aristocratic family, and that included the illegitimate child of a baron. They had gone on to do well for themselves in the local area, and they were all keenly aware of the importance of respectability, net curtains, and giving a good impression. She would never have wanted people to know that she had married a man who wanted to have sex with other men, and who had never really loved her in the first place. What would the neighbours have thought? Grandma and Grandad had used money to buy respectability when they couldn't get it any other way. If there were problems, they threw money at them until they went away or were brushed under the carpet. Grandad paid the men he slept with to keep them quiet. When he beat Grandma up, she just stayed in the house until the bruises had gone down. They both slipped Mum some extra money for the housekeeping if she complained about Dad's violence, and advised her not to report Dad to the police because he was just sensitive and he didn't really mean it. They both stressed to Mum that she should never leave Dad, because then they wouldn't help her out financially anymore and, with three kids to take care of, she would be on her own and in a very vulnerable situation. For really big problems, they could donate some cash to their friend Cyril Smith's political campaigns, and he would make sure they went away. Cyril, a larger-than life character who had never married and lived with his mother, was a prominent local figure who served as MP for the Liberal Democrats and then the Conservatives. I remember conversations about how Dad had had "breakdowns" and done things he didn't really mean. With a bit of cash here, and a nod and a wink there, Dad's misdeeds were brushed under the carpet, along with all the rest of the family secrets.

***

"At least the old man was good for something," Dad said happily when he learned that he had inherited £30,000, "I thought he might have spent it all on that bloody Steven by now."

Grandad had done his best to spend Grandma's money after she passed away, but he had died before he could get through it and now it was all Dad's. £30,000 was a significant windfall. Dad could have spent some of it on doing up the house or propping up the business, but he behaved as though he had just won the lotto. He'd come home after work, put on one of his clean shirts, and head out into the night to spend it on booze and prostitutes and impressing his friends by buying a round for everyone in the bar. You can get through a lot of money very quickly that way. Mum was humiliated. Dad didn't even try to hide the fact that he was spending his money on prostitutes, and everyone knew that he didn't care about his family. Mum felt that she had failed as a wife, and blamed herself for much of his behaviour, because he was always telling her that she was inadequate in many ways. She was so bitter about how her married life had turned out, she couldn't see that she was also failing as a mother. Her own misery had grown so immense that her children's misery was not even visible to her most of the time.

***

Although I was bullied and had few friends – certainly no boys – I did find a lifeline in my friendship with a number of the girls in my class. They didn't care that I was a "poof" and "walked funny", but seemed to feel comfortable around me, perhaps because they knew that I had no ulterior motive in seeking them out, unlike most of the boys their age. Lisa, Amy, Wendy and I were in the same classes. We all took family studies and cooking, and after school we sometimes went to one of their houses (never mine; I would not have wanted to expose any of them to the possibility that Dad would molest or leer at them) to hang out and chat about the latest pop hits or our favourite soap stars over tea and biscuits. None of them ever asked me anything about my family, but I am sure that they knew that things were not easy for me at home, and certainly they were all aware of Grandad and what he had done. It was a small community, and everybody knew that Dad was difficult, too. The girls could also see that I was struggling at school, especially in English Lit, and they did their best to help me get through the exams. We went over and over *Of Mice and Men* until I was almost able to get to grips with it. If I could see those girls now, I would thank them from the bottom of my heart, because they made high school almost bearable, and provided some moments of sanity in a life that was often hell. If it hadn't been for them, I would probably have taken my own life. My suicidal fantasies continued – when I wasn't practicing jumping down the last few stairs and trying to work up my courage to throw myself down the whole flight, I was lying with my head under the duvet, hoping that I would run out of oxygen and pass away quietly in the night.

***

When I was about sixteen, I came home from school one day to find Mum in tears in the kitchen. She was sitting hunched over the table, her shoulders heaving, and Dad was brandishing a copy of the local newspaper at her.

"Bet you're not feeling so horny now!" he said. "Eh, Bev?"

"Stop it, Ron, just stop," she sobbed.

"Why should I stop when you just rub it in my face every single fucking day of our lives? Why should I stop when our whole marriage has involved my charity to your offspring?"

A local man had been killed in a car accident, and the newspaper had covered the accident. He was a businessman from the area, now sadly missed by his wife and children. He was also the love of my mother's life and – although he didn't know it yet – Jason's biological father. Shortly after their marriage, Mum had had an affair and become pregnant. The father of the child had not wanted anything to do with her, and just went on with his happy marriage and family life as though nothing had happened. All this time, Dad had been exerting power over Mum because he had been man enough to take her back, despite the fact that she had – as he called it – a bastard child.

Mum and Dad's marriage had always been a mess, but now it got worse. He blatantly paraded the sad, ugly girls he was sleeping with in front of us all, and acquired a steady girlfriend called Dawn. Mum despised Dawn, and referred to her as "Dawn the Yawn." But Dad thought she was fun. Dawn liked to dress up for him and was happy to indulge all his sexual whims, no matter how ridiculous. I remember her perched on his knee in a Santa Claus outfit at Christmas time, drunk and giggling.

"We're out of here!" Mum would shout, dragging me and Daniel away from Dad's shop when she found him with Dawn or one of his other women. "I don't have to stay here and be humiliated by you!"

Dad would just laugh. Back at home, Mum raged and wept, but she had learned enough to know that it didn't make any difference what she said and did. She may have suspected that some of Dad's girls were under the age of consent, but if she did, she never said anything about it. So far as she could see, Dad had decided that he had a right to do whatever he wanted, and there was nothing she could do about it.

After Dawn, Dad picked up another steady girlfriend, a young girl called Mandy who was friendly with a girlfriend of Jason's. Despite her young age (she had just left school), Mandy was working locally as a prostitute. She had problems with drugs and alcohol and was raising two children on her own. Prostitution was common in the area, largely because there were quite high rates of poverty, and young girls from difficult family backgrounds often had friends or older female relatives who were already on the game and could show them the ropes. There were also plenty of men like Dad, prepared to spend the housekeeping money on sex.

Not despite, but because of, this behaviour, the men in Dad's group of friends seemed to think that he was some kind of a hero. They were all greasy perverts like him, but they weren't as brave as he was about letting it all hang out. They used to hang around the shop reading porn magazines, and often came to our house in the evenings.

"I don't know how you do it, Ron," they would say admiringly. "You've got women eating out of the palm of your hand."

Dad would make Mum serve his friends food and drink while they watched telly and talked about screwing girls and cheating on their long-suffering wives and bragged about getting their hands on porno tapes so extreme they were illegal. While Mum was handing around the snacks, Dad boasted about how he was never going to be caught getting another woman knocked up, because he had had a vasectomy: "I'm shooting blanks, boys. They're not getting any money out of me that way."

Mum's mouth would tighten when he started talking about those things, but there was nothing she could do, and she kept right on handing around cans of beer and bowls of crisps.

We all knew about Dad's vasectomy because it hadn't gone well, leaving him in considerable pain for a number of months. There had been a lot of shouting, cursing, and heavy drinking until he felt better.

While the vasectomy meant that Dad was not going to have any more children, he was now even more careless about his sexual health than he had been before and didn't think twice about "sticking it in anyone," as Mum put it. He frequently picked up venereal diseases, and passed them on to Mum, until our family GP must have been sick of the sight of them both.

"Your dad doesn't believe in condoms," Mum said, "and there is nothing I can do about it."

***

Because of the chaos going on around me, I found it very difficult to understand what was right and what was wrong. Dad was so blasé about the girls he messed around with in the shop and on his market stall. It made me feel uncomfortable seeing him like that, and I could see that it made Mum angry, but it took me a long time to understand that what he was doing was wrong. Mum confided everything in me, telling me things about my father and his sex life that no child or young person should ever have to know. When I did start to realise that aspects of my family life were not just stressful, but immoral and even criminal, I promised myself that I would never let myself behave the way my father did, and that I would always try to do the exact opposite. This realisation helped me to start nourishing the first tiny shoots of an identity of my own.

Chapter Five: Growing Up

Although several of my teachers had encouraged me to stay in school to do A-levels, and told me that I could achieve more if I only applied myself, I never managed to really engage with my studies, and left school with just mediocre grades in a few GCSEs. I wasn't sure what I wanted to do with my life, and had little confidence in my ability to achieve anything meaningful, but in the meanwhile I got a job at the local Tesco.

Work was simple and repetitive, but it was a great relief to be away from the nastiness and bullying of school. My colleagues seemed to like me, and it was rewarding going to work every day, seeing smiling faces, and not having to put up with people calling me ugly names because they thought I was a "faggot". I began to feel slightly hopeful for the future. I worked hard, hoping to impress the boss and have the opportunity to move up in the company.

***

By the time I turned seventeen, Mum and Dad's marriage was collapsing. It had always been marked by shouting, alcoholism, and abuse, but now it was finally falling apart completely.

"Mum," I said one day, after a lot of thought, "you've got to leave him. You can't go on like this. He'll end up killing you."

"I can't," she said. "What would I do, and where would I go?"

Over a period of a few months, I persuaded Mum that she would be OK without Dad because I would step in and provide for her. I was working full time and making just enough to pay the rent on a small house where Mum, Daniel, and I could finally be safe from Dad's rampages. She would qualify for benefits, and between us we would manage.

"I'll look after you," I promised. "I've got a job and I can pay the rent on a house."

"Do you know what you are taking on?" Mum said. She made it sound more like a threat than a question.

"Yes," I told her, "and I'm up for it."

At seventeen, I actually had no idea what I was letting myself in for. All I knew was that I wanted the nightmare of living with Dad to end, and that I felt a sense of responsibility for my mother and her well-being and happiness. Mum, Daniel and I moved out and into the tiny house that was all I could afford. Dad acted like he didn't care, but he had just experienced a big blow to his self-esteem. Despite the fact that he slept around like a tomcat, he had liked to know that Mum was back at the house and dependent on him, no matter what sort of treatment he meted out to her.

Leaving Dad brought me a great sense of relief, but the knowledge that I was now responsible for my mother was terrifying. My OCD got worse and worse, and it extended to an obsession that meant I had to hear everything repeated several times before I could believe it. When I asked Mum a question, I made sure she answered it over and over again until I finally experienced a sense of peace. She never questioned what I was doing, but simply answered my questions like some sort of automaton. In retrospect, I can see that I had become addicted to the repetitions. They gave me a kick. By never challenging me in any way, Mum was like a dealer, enabling a psychological habit that was anything but healthy. I went to the GP about the OCD, but he didn't help at all.

"To be honest, Nick," he said. "I don't think there's anything wrong with you other than an overactive imagination."

The doctor prescribed a short course of anti-depressants and told me to pull myself together.

"You're a healthy young man and there's nothing wrong with you," he said. "You've just got to buck up."

The GP was the same one I had been attending since childhood. He had seen my brothers and me through all our childhood illnesses and numerous cuts and bruises. He had treated Mum and

Dad for venereal disease, and had dressed Mum's wounds from yet another beating. I suspect that he had written us off as just another problem family, and felt that I was only looking for attention.

After a year in rented accommodation, I decided to get a mortgage and buy a small house where I would live with Mum and Daniel. I found a small terraced house with two bedrooms for £30,000 and took out a mortgage. We all moved in and tried to make it feel like home.

I thought that Mum would be grateful for all the effort I had gone to, but she was passive and non-committal.

"It's very small," she said with a sniff. "But beggars can't be choosers."

I had hoped that owning my own property would make me feel more secure, but instead I became progressively more anxious. The GP prescribed some more tablets. They didn't seem to help, and having them in the house offered the possibility of using them to kill myself – I still had fantasies about ending my life. When Mum realised this, she flushed them all down the toilet.

"And don't go back down to the doctor looking for more," she said. "I've had enough of drugs with your father. I don't want to see you going down the same road."

I had promised Mum that I would take care of her, and I took my promise seriously, although I was just eighteen and barely able to take care of myself. Thinking that she would be happier if she was more independent, and that she might get a job and learn how to support herself, I put her through driving lessons and bought her a car. Thinking that she might be happier if she felt loved and appreciated, I paid for her to go on holiday. It was all a stretch on my salary from the supermarket, and I had to get out a loan to fund these expenses. Not having worked all her adult life, Mum did not seem to understand how difficult it was for me to scrape together the money I needed to get her things. She took them, but often complained about her standard of living, and how there were so many things that we could not afford.

When I confided in Nan that I was under financial pressure because of all the things I was doing for Mum, she snorted.

"Well," she said, "it was *your* idea for her to leave him in the first place, so now you are responsible for taking care of her. If you break it, you own it. I never thought that she should have left him in the first place. In my day, marriage was for life, and if you didn't like it, you had to lump it."

"But Nan," I said, "he was vicious. He used to beat her up all the time."

"Well," said Nan. "She should have thought of that in first place. And I've always said that the only thing wrong with a man who beats his wife is that he's not managed properly. If she had made a bigger effort to control him, it would never have happened. She's weak and doesn't know her own mind; that's her problem."

I begged Mum to consider getting a job. While she hadn't worked outside the home since her marriage, she was still relatively young, and if I could stack shelves in a supermarket, so could she.

"What's the point, Nick?" she said. "Nobody would want to hire me, not with the little bit of work experience I have. And anyway, your brother is too young and needs me at home. I would be letting him down if I went out to work. I'm not going to do that to him."

Daniel, who was nearly as tall as I was, was just about to start secondary school. I felt that he could easily have managed without a mother at home full-time and that it would be good for him to see her getting back on her feet and becoming more independent. Daniel was really clever, we could all see that, but from Mum he had picked up the idea that the world owed him a living and that he didn't need to make any effort of his own. I thought that if Mum showed Daniel by example that anyone could get off their bum and get a job, it might be easier for him to get on in life in a few years' time. But Mum was immovable. She added that she thought she was starting to get arthritis, and that doing a job would make her symptoms worse. She fretted that if she worked for a while and then decided to stop, it might be too difficult to get back on the benefits that she relied on. After a while, I realised that she had no intention of ever going to work and stopped trying to persuade her.

***

My first consensual sexual relationship was with a colleague at work called Dave. Dave was married to Carol, who also worked at the supermarket. They were both in their thirties, and it was obvious that Dave had married Carol because he was not comfortable with his sexual identity; he had lived with his elderly mother until she died, using her illness as the excuse he needed not to deal with his sexuality and the adult world of love and relationships. The façade he had constructed came tumbling down around him when Carol came home and found the two of us in bed together. We had been working the Sunday night shift together, and had spent the following Monday drinking in the pub. As I was not used to drinking, I got drunk very quickly, and Dave saw his chance and moved in on me. While I wasn't especially attracted to him, I was flattered by the attention, and reciprocated eagerly. Carol was understandably very upset when she caught us in the act. There was a huge show-down between Carol and

Dave while I dragged on my clothes and left. Neither of them turned up at work the next day. I felt that I had done nothing to be ashamed of, as I had not cheated on anybody, and came to work as usual, by which stage Carol had confided in her friends, and everyone at work had heard on the grapevine about what had happened.

"Good on you," my colleagues said when they saw me. "We didn't think you'd have the guts to turn up."

The whole thing was quite the scandal among the supermarket staff for a few days, and I had to brazen it out and put up with a lot of ribald jokes. The one good thing that came out of my liaison with Dave was that I was now officially out of the closet and didn't have to lie any more, to myself or to anybody else.

When I told Mum that I was gay, she was supportive: "So long as you are happy, son." I am sure that, on some level, she had always known.

"Shall I tell Dad, if I bump into him around town?" she asked. "Maybe he should know. He's your father, after all."

"I don't care," I said. "Tell him if you want, or don't. It doesn't make any difference to me."

Dad had been calling me a "poof" for years, anyway, so what difference would it make?

When Nan found out that I was gay, she professed sadness, even though she had never seemed to like me.

"If there was a pill you could take that would cure you, I'd give it to you," Nan said. "It's not a good way to live."

"Well, there isn't," I told her. "So you're just going to have to get used to it."

"It's such a shame," she said. "You're a nice-looking boy and it is just a waste. And think of all the nasty diseases. I blame your mother; she's a weak woman and she's passed the weakness on to you."

I didn't want to talk to a bigoted old lady about my sexuality, and from then on, we avoided the topic and managed to remain civil.

***

Back in the mid-nineties, Manchester had a lively nightlife, and I was delighted to be part of it. I went to the Gay Village every Friday and Saturday night. When men found me attractive, I basked in the attention and started to feel a little better about myself. Soon I had a small group of friends – Tony, Jason, and Richard – who were gay, like me, and I realised that I was very far from being alone. There were thousands of us. We came from every sort of social background and did every sort of job. We were old, young, and in between. There was nothing wrong with me. I was a normal, healthy, young gay man. I hoped that one day I would meet someone I could really love.

The gay scene in Manchester was just amazing. The main street in the gay village, which overlooked one of Manchester's many canals, was lined with bars, with bubbly pop music pouring out of them: Kylie, Steps, and all the dance tunes of the day. They were lit up with fairy lights and LED lights that reflected in the canal, and decorated with bubble tubes featuring coloured lights and water. Everyone was happy, everyone was excited, and everyone was just having a good time until the early hours of the morning. As I often didn't drink – I didn't really like to have too much because I didn't enjoy the sensation of being out of control, and, anyway, I couldn't afford it on what I earned at the supermarket – I could ferry people home at the end of the evening. In return, I had a group of men who were there to give me advice and support. I remember them taking me out shopping and showing me where to buy aftershave and clothes that flattered my figure. I didn't have a lot of money to spend, but I did what I could.

Still eighteen, I fell seriously in love for the first time. Through work, I had made some friends, including a local man who was a regular customer. I had a bit of a social life with them in my home area and through this was introduced to Rob, who was in his early thirties. I was always most attracted to older men, and I fell hard for Rob, who was handsome and well-dressed, and seemed to ooze confidence out of every pore. Soon I was going around to his house all the time.

"Who's this Rob, then?" Mum asked curiously. "You seem to be with him all the time, but I've never even seen him."

I didn't want her to ruin what I felt I had with Rob, so I didn't tell her how much he mattered to me.

"He's just a friend," I said. "Someone I know from work."

But I had really fallen for Rob and was allowing myself to imagine the life we might have together. I was impressed by all he had achieved. Rob had a good job as a civil servant in the council, and he owned his own house. He took care of himself, looked good, and could afford a comfortable standard of living. Staying with him gave me a welcome break from taking care of Mum and Daniel, and I began to think that maybe this was the one, and that we would move in together.

After about nine months, Rob got tired of my clinginess and dumped me unceremoniously. I was absolutely heartbroken when I realised that all the time I had been playing happy families with Rob, for him it had always been about the sex, and not much else. I was devastated. I had really believed that Rob would be the one, my Prince Charming, who would pluck me out of my miserable family and make me happy. I was so distraught, I couldn't eat or drink and lost weight. I sat in my room crying, and was not always able to go to work. All I could think of was the dream of a better future that I had just lost.

"What the hell is wrong with you?" Mum said. "You're responsible for the family now. Get your finger out and do something. Who is going to pay the rent if you don't go to work? Remember that Daniel and I are here because of you; we'd never have left your father if you hadn't said you'd take care of everything."

I kept ringing Rob's number, hoping that he would pick up the phone so that I could hear his voice.

"Let it go," my friends advised. "He's just like that. He picks up younger men for sex and when he gets bored with them, he cuts them off. You're not the first and you won't be the last. He's not worth it. You deserve better."

"No," I insisted. "What we had was really special and I just want him to realise it."

At first, I was sure that Rob had really loved me and that if only I could get through to him and show him how strongly I felt about our relationship, we would get back together and everything would be OK. Eventually, I realised that my friends were right and that I had just been a piece of tail; just another notch on Rob's bedpost. I felt that I had been abused, chewed up and spat out and, on some level, I have never forgiven Rob for the hurt he caused me as a vulnerable young man in love for the first time. I can see how he was stifled by my youthful enthusiasm, but it wouldn't have killed him to let me down more easily.

Reeling from a broken heart, on the rebound I became involved with another man, Neil, who was about twenty years older than me. Neil was kind in many ways, and tried to help me to deal with the OCD that was still a big problem for me, but between the age-gap and my neediness, after less than a year he had had enough too. We were on holiday in Cyprus when he dumped me unceremoniously, leaving us awkwardly sharing the private villa he had borrowed from a friend and sitting together on the flight on the way back. The truth was, we had never had anything in common.

***

Mum was curious about my new life and my experiences in the gay village, and she was accepting of my sexuality, but I never introduced her to my gay friends, and certainly not to the few men I had serious relationships with. My parents had spoiled so many things for me in the course of my short life, and I didn't want her to wreck the one aspect of my existence that I was actually comfortable with. And the sad truth is that I was embarrassed by my mother and our home life. It wasn't about her appearance, because she was still taking care of herself then. It was more about her reluctance to do anything to make things better. I had the only salary in the house, and Mum was addicted to her benefits, which she could still claim because Daniel was fifteen and in full-time education. She had no sense that maybe she should contribute actively to the household, and seemed determined to remain a passive victim of Dad, even though we had finally managed to get away from him. She blamed everyone but herself for the situation she was in. I didn't want my friends to see our home, and realise that, even though I was the main provider, I had to share a bedroom with my little brother.

Although Mum said that she couldn't work because she needed to be there for Daniel, she was failing him badly as a mother. Daniel had always been bright in his own way, but he had disengaged completely from school. He had been attending special classes that were supposed to help him get up to speed with the academic subjects, but they had marked him out as a target for bullies, and he was having a very difficult time. The school welfare officer came to the house, but things never got any better. In fact, Daniel stopped going to school altogether. Teachers came by with work for him to do at home, coaxing and cajoling him to at least do a few GCSEs. Daniel was having none of it. He refused to go to school and all Mum did was shrug and say that there was nothing she could do about it, as he had made up his mind.

"He's a big lad now," she said. "I can't drag him to school."

I couldn't help thinking again that if Mum provided a better example for Daniel, by actually going out and doing something herself, he might be more inclined to get off his own arse.

***

Just when I was starting to feel good about myself, my appearance and my sexuality, I hit a major setback. One night, somewhat the worse for wear for drink, I agreed to go back to someone's house. When I got there, it was clear that he wanted sex and felt that by going home with him I had promised to deliver. I didn't, but he wasn't taking no for an answer, and as he was much bigger than I was, he just held me down and raped me while I cried out in pain. Afterwards, I blamed myself for having had too much to drink and for going back to his house. I didn't think that anyone would believe me, because I was a sexually active gay man, so I just went to the clinic for a check-up. Thankfully, he had worn a condom and I was OK. I never discussed the assault with anybody and I certainly never considered reporting it to the police. I was sure that they would not care.

Not long after that, I got involved in a relationship with a man called Mark. While I didn't fall as hard for him as I had for Rob, I liked and felt comfortable with him. Mark was older than me, good-looking, and comfortably off. He said that he loved me, and I believed him. I began to think that maybe Mark was the one who would provide me with the security I longed for.

One night, Mark was drinking with a friend of his called Spiro, a Greek guy who lived in Manchester. Spiro invited us both up to his apartment. When we got there, Mark and Spiro started doing drugs, starting with hash brownies and then moving on to the hard stuff. This was not my scene, and I felt very uncomfortable. Then things got out of hand. Mark and Spiro were laughing and joking about me, and Mark told Spiro that he should tie me up in the bedroom.

"What's going on?" I asked.

"It's OK, Nick," Mark said. "I am right here in the next room. I won't let anything happen to you."

I let Spiro tie me up because Mark had said that it was OK. I felt uncomfortable about the situation, but I also felt a sense of obligation to do what Mark said, because he was my boyfriend, he was older than me, and I thought he loved me.

Spiro tied me up, pulled down my clothes, and raped me while I called out for Mark to help. The whole time, Mark just sat in the next room, ignoring my cries. He thought it was all extremely entertaining and, when Spiro was done, he asked me if I had had a nice time.

When it was all over and I had been untied, I got into the bath and sat there, sobbing my eyes out. Again, I blamed myself for being raped. How could I have allowed it to happen again? What was wrong with me? What was I doing that provoked men to behave in such a way? It was only later that I understood that Mark had never really cared for me at all, and that this had been part of the plan the whole time. Mark had a lot more in common with Dad than I had ever realised. I had been the young bait that he had used to attract Spiro.

The dark side of the gay village in Manchester in the nineties was the fact that there were a lot of older men acting like predators, picking up younger men, buying them drinks and presents, and waiting until they felt safe and secure before taking advantage of, or even assaulting, them. Mark had been like a gay version of my father, and I had been the vulnerable young person whom he had taken advantage of. I had long looked down on the poor, silly girls that Dad had fooled around with, but now I could see that I wasn't really very different to them. Like them, I came from a difficult family background and found it hard to know who to trust. Like them, I suffered from low self-esteem and was vulnerable to flattery and the suggestion that someone wanted to take care of me. Like them, I could be tempted to use my young body to get approving attention from an older person who seemed to care.

I was sure that nobody cared about same-sex assault. We had all heard that the police didn't believe gay men who said that they had been raped, and that even if they did believe them, they didn't do anything. Rape cases rarely, if ever, even made it to court. There was little or no awareness among the victims that this wasn't OK and that they had a right to be safe. Everyone was drinking and a lot of people were taking drugs. The occasional rape victim seemed to be the price that society just had to pay for a more visible gay culture.

A few days after the second assault, I called my friends and they helped me move all my stuff out of Mark's house. They knew what had happened to me, but they didn't say anything. What was there to say? They had seen it all before.

***

I decided to focus on my career for a while, and put myself in for management training. I enjoyed my work at Tesco, but I didn't want to be stacking shelves for the rest of my life. Two problems emerged. Firstly, I was still dealing with OCD, which was enabled and reinforced at home with every interaction with my mother. Secondly, I was told in no uncertain terms that there was a limit to how far I would go in the supermarket chain, because the powers that be would not like to see a gay man moving up the management ladder. I seriously doubt that this was the actual policy at the organisation, but my area manager was a homophobe, and completely open about it.

I decided that I had had enough, left Tesco and went to work at a home for people with disabilities of various kinds. I felt comfortable with care work because of my experience with my second cousin Sean, and because I had been taking care of my mother all my life.

***

When I turned twenty-one, I decided that it was time for me to treat myself for once, and I blew all the money I had on a three-week holiday in the Caribbean. It was beautiful, and I had a holiday romance with a handsome Spanish man who gave my ego a boost. Away from the daily grind, I had time to think about what I really wanted from my life. When I came home, I decided that I didn't want to be my mother's caretaker any more, and put the house on the market.

"I can't believe you're doing this to us!" Mum screeched. "You are making us homeless. You might as well get all our stuff and just throw it out onto the street. And have you even given a thought to what you are doing to Daniel? He is still practically a child!"

"I'm not your husband!" I shouted back. "You are an adult woman and you are not my responsibility! I've had enough of being told that I have to take care of you and Daniel."

"I would never have left Ron if it wasn't for you. This is all your fault!"

"If you hadn't left him, you'd probably be dead by now, you silly woman."

By the time things got so bad that Mum was rushing at me with the breadknife, I knew that I had to move on.

Although I knew I was doing the right thing, I could understand where Mum's fury was coming from. She was still drinking heavily, and she felt hopeless and lost. As a wife and mother, she had been utterly dependent on Dad for years, and she had forgotten how to live on her own. She was scared of taking a risk and getting a job, because Dad had destroyed her self-esteem so effectively that she was sure she would fail at everything.

Because the sale of the house effectively made her homeless, Mum went to the top of the housing list and was quickly given a council flat for her and Daniel to live in. She could not afford to be particular, and the flat was awful; a real dump that nobody could have made look like home.

I felt bad for Mum, but relieved that I had finally made the decision to cut her loose. I wished her all the best, but I had finally realised that it was not my job to take care of her. She remained angry with me for a while, but eventually relented somewhat and we started to talk again, although I tried to maintain some distance for the sake of my own sanity.

To tell the truth, I think that Mum and Dad would have split up even if I had not precipitated it. Dad had been involved with Mandy even before the separation, and she was named in the divorce that followed shortly after their separation as one of the reasons for it. When Mum left, Dad continued to see Mandy, who went on with her chaotic lifestyle of drugs and drink. I can only imagine that the men that Mandy encountered must have been really horrendous for her to choose to remain in a relationship with Dad, and even go on holiday with him. After a while, we found out that they had gone their separate ways. I can only hope that she and her children were not too badly scarred by their experience of living with him.

***

Liberated from looking after Mum and Daniel, and finally free from Dad's influence, I decided that I would take care of myself and put myself first for change. Maybe my dream of finding someone special – a kind man, older than me – falling in love, and being cared for would even come true. It didn't seem likely, but who knew? Maybe the love of my life was right around the corner.

Chapter Six: Love and Retribution

At twenty-one, I was still struggling with OCD and with the traumatic effects of both my abusive childhood and the sexual assaults that I had suffered while I was still coming to terms with my sexuality. I was determined to build a good life for myself, but I often felt as though I didn't know how, and that there were many obstacles in my way. Most of all, despite some unhappy experiences with relationships, I wanted to meet someone special and settle down, and I had faith that maybe one day this would be possible. Just because my parents' marriage had been a disaster didn't mean, I hoped, that I could never be happy. I imagined that one day I would meet the right person, and then everything would change for the better. I hoped that I deserved to have some good things happen in my life.

Then I met Tony. I had joined a local gym, planning to get fitter and stronger, and I noticed a handsome guy in the jacuzzi one day in December 2001. I introduced myself and struck up conversation with him, asking if he had any exciting plans for the weekend, and hoping that his answer would give me some insight into his living situation at home. Was he gay? Straight? Married? Single? It was impossible to tell, but I was very anxious to find out.

"I'm going out," he said, without giving any more details. "Just a normal evening out."

He added that his name was "Tony" but didn't have much else to contribute. Well, that didn't leave me any the wiser. At least I knew his name, though.

Tony and I met at the gym a few times, by which stage my gaydar was telling me clearly that he was gay, which was a good start. Our conversation progressed to exchanging a little more information about ourselves, and as I deduced that he was single, I started working myself up towards asking if he would like to meet me for coffee one day.

Then an accident at work meant I couldn't attend the gym for a couple of months while I recovered. When I finally went back in February, Tony was still there. I wasn't well enough to exercise yet, just to go to the spa, but thankfully Tony was waiting. Seeing him after a hiatus of two months, I realised that he was special, and that I wanted, more than anything, to get to know him.

"Would you like to go out for a drink?" I asked Tony one day, having plucked up my courage. To my delight, he said that he would. Our date went better than I could have imagined. The conversation flowed, and towards the end of the evening, Tony said that he had a confession to make.

"What is it?" I asked, hoping that he was not going to tell me that he was already married.

"Well, the last two months I've been going to the gym every day at different times, hoping to run into you. I've been kicking myself for not asking you out before, and I was giving up hope of ever seeing you again."

Before long, Tony and I were in a serious, committed relationship and all my dreams had come true.

Older than me, with a senior position in the Greater Manchester Police, Tony had been out of the closet socially, if not at work, for a number of years, since the end of his marriage to a woman. We became close quickly, so much so that Tony was the first person I ever told, other than Mum and the police, about the abuse I had suffered at my grandfather's hands. In fact, I told him everything about my family, and he understood. Getting it all off my chest was therapeutic in and of itself. As I spoke, I was torn between my fear that Tony would be revolted when he knew the truth about my family, and a sense of relief that I was finally letting it all out.

"Look, Nick," Tony told me, "above all, I want you to know that you're much more than just a victim. Despite your awful childhood, you have picked yourself up, got a job, and you're able to support yourself with no help from anyone."

Tony pointed out to me that the fact that I had survived showed that I have resilience.

"I know you're still struggling in some ways," he said, referring to my OCD, "but we can work through it together and, because you are strong and resourceful, you will come out the other side."

Where Mum had tolerated and indulged my OCD, including my need to have my questions answered over and over again, Tony challenged me.

"No," he would say, "I've already answered your question once, and I know you heard me. I'm not going to repeat myself."

Gradually, we were able to work together to conquer the lingering effects of my traumatic childhood.

I had always blamed myself for the sexual assaults I had suffered as a young adult, after I had come out of the closet. I thought that they were my fault because I had been drinking, because I had been naïve, and because I must have been sending out the wrong signals, or not saying "no" loud enough or often enough. When I told Tony about what had happened, he hugged me tightly.

"Being raped is *never* the victims' fault," he said. "Just like it wasn't your fault when your grandfather molested you. The fact that you had been drinking, or that you might have made some foolish decisions, doesn't make you culpable. The only person to blame when someone is raped is the rapist. Never forget it. You can't let the actions of another person destroy your life."

One night, Tony and I were out for a drink in Manchester and we bumped into Mark, who had given me to Spiro to be assaulted and sat in the next room while it happened. I pointed him out to Tony, who went over and told him that he knew all about what had happened, and that if he ever came near me again, he would regret it. In that moment, I truly understood that my dreams of finding someone who would love and protect me had come true, and that Tony was that man.

I was working as a carer in the community at this time for eight people who lived with serious mental health issues and whose homes were publicly subsidised flats. While I struggled to maintain distance with Mum and Daniel, it was different with my clients because they were not family, and I could remain objective about their situations and needs. I enjoyed the work and found it rewarding to know that I could make a positive difference in the lives of people who faced so many challenges – and I experienced a sense of "there but for the grace of God go I".

***

While things were getting better for me, Mum and Daniel were still dealing with the after-effects of their long, abusive relationship with Dad. Daniel, who had dropped out of school completely by now, stopped eating and drinking. The weight fell off him, and Mum got seriously concerned about him.

"You've got to do something, Nick," Mum said every time she phoned. "I just can't cope with him anymore. You've got to stand up and take some responsibility for this. You're his brother, for God's sake. You can't just stand back and let him starve himself to death!"

While I had been trying to maintain some distance between Mum and me, I felt awful for Daniel, and I could hear how distressed Mum was about him. I often didn't agree with how Mum chose to deal with Daniel's many problems, but I knew that she loved him and wanted the best for him. That's all I wanted for him, too. I went over to the house as often as I could, begging and pleading with Daniel to eat and drink. He was in such distress that nothing seemed to make any difference, and I sometimes wondered if he could even hear me. At that point, Daniel was so wrapped up in his own misery that he seemed to be incapable of doing anything to help himself. He was completely unable to express whatever was going on in his mind. He just shook his head and refused to engage with me at all.

A few weeks after Daniel's self-imposed hunger strike had started, Mum called me at work to let me know that he had taken a turn for the worse.

"He's been admitted to hospital," she sobbed. "He's really sick. The doctors say that he could die."

I rushed to the hospital and found a terribly underweight Daniel in bed. He looked awful. He had been given multiple blood transfusions and was on a drip to rehydrate him. Mum sat by his bed wringing her hands. When the doctors came by to see who was the responsible adult, she didn't even look at them, and they quickly realised that she was not going to be much help. As the nearest available relative prepared to engage with his healthcare providers, once again it was all up to me. Over the next few weeks, I saw Daniel's therapist, his dietician, his doctor, and all the nurses on the ward. They all learned quickly that there was no point talking to Mum. I was just twenty-two years old, and everyone was expecting me to stand up and take responsibility for Daniel as though I were his father. My stomach in a knot with stress, I felt that there was nothing I could do but get on with it.

2002 was my first Christmas with Tony, and we had hoped to do all the traditional things together, but I spent it at hospital with Daniel. Mum came in, but it was obvious that she was drinking heavily again.

"What's going on with you, Mum?" I asked, exasperated. "Daniel is sick and he needs to be looked after. This is not the right time for you to start hitting the bottle."

"You're here, aren't you?" she said. "Why can't you do it?"

When I went home that day, I was exhausted and upset.

"How am I supposed to have a normal career and a decent life when I'm over at Mum's taking care of her and Daniel the whole time?" I asked Tony. "I'm a carer at work all day, and then I have to go back over to theirs and do it all again. She's not even trying to take care of herself, let alone Daniel, and she's back on the booze."

"You *don't* have to do it," Tony said simply. "You can just stop. You don't have to stop loving them, but you are not responsible for them. You can decide to stand back and let them start taking care of themselves for a change."

Fortunately, Daniel responded to treatment, started eating and drinking normally, and was allowed to go home. I was happy that he was better, but envisioned a future in which Mum rang me every single time something went wrong, and demanded that I fix it. I knew that if I let things continue the way they were, I would spend my life trying – and inevitably failing – to keep Mum and Daniel happy and safe. In the process, I would risk destroying my own chance at happiness.

Because I was finally in a happy relationship with someone who loved and respected me, I had more self-esteem than ever before. I talked with Tony about the situation with Daniel, and we both came to the conclusion that, while he was my brother and I would always be available to help him to an appropriate extent, it was not fair for me to have to be his parent, too. I needed to focus on finding my own way in the world rather than dealing with one family crisis after another. I needed to gain some distance from Mum and Daniel, and learn how to put myself first.

"I can't keep caring for him," I told Mum. "I love Daniel, but I am not his father; I'm his brother. It's not my job to tell him how to shave or to nag him to have a shower and stay clean. It's *your* job. I have to take care of myself."

"I can't believe you're treating us like this," Mum snuffled. "It's like you just don't care. Things aren't easy for me, you know. It's all very well for you, with your job and your friends and all that, but I have nothing and nobody. It's not fair. I would never have left your father if it wasn't for you."

I felt sorry for her, but increasingly impatient. She had been through hell with Dad, but had never done anything to help herself, and seemed to have no intention of doing so now. She could have seen a counsellor on the NHS, but she wouldn't even countenance the idea. She could have got some training and gone to work, but she insisted that Daniel needed her at home – and then she didn't even take care of Daniel, who was losing the plot. I could see that she was in a fragile emotional state, and I wished that I could wave a wand and make everything magically better, but I had had enough of compromising my own mental well-being to take care of everybody else.

"You've got to prioritise yourself," Tony told me. "You've spent your whole life trying to take care of your family at your own expense; now you need to take care of yourself for the first time. I'm not prepared to sit here and watch you make yourself ill by worrying about things that shouldn't be your problem at all. Besides, I know you think that you are doing your best for her, but when you swoop in and solve all her problems, you're making it harder for her to ever learn how to stand on her own two feet. If she's never challenged, she'll never figure out how to do things differently, and things will just stay the same forever."

I could not find the words to express to Mum how I felt, so Tony wrote her a letter, making it clear that her behaviour was having a terrible impact on my quality of life, and that it was time I drew some clear boundaries that would allow me to focus on my own needs.

"Who's this Tony, then?" Mum asked, brandishing his letter when I went to visit shortly afterwards. "Who the hell does he think he is, writing to me and telling me how to live my life?"

"Tony's my boyfriend, Mum," I said. "I already told you about him. You know perfectly well that we are in a serious relationship. He cares about me. He just wants what's best for me because he loves me."

"Well, you can tell him where to shove his letter, because these are *his* words and thoughts, not yours, and I don't believe a word of it. I'm your mother and I can tell when you are being manipulated. *My* Nick would never say anything like this to me! The boy I raised would not turn his back on his mother and brother in their hour of need. He's manipulating you and turning you against your own family. He's a bad man."

"Actually, Mum," I said. "Tony has just expressed what I have been trying to tell you for years, and haven't had the courage to express. It's not fair, expecting me to do everything. I'm your son, not your husband or your father. I need to focus on my own life."

I understood that I was not actually doing Mum any favours by endlessly going over to her place to sort out the mess. I told her that I would be available to her when she finally felt ready to help herself, but that until then she was on her own. It was incredibly difficult to make that decision and say those words, but as soon as I did, I felt as though an immense weight had been lifted from me. I finally understood that there was nothing wrong with prioritising myself for a while.

**

After a year as a couple, Tony and I decided to move in together and I packed up all my stuff and brought it to his apartment. Shortly after that, Tony had a serious car accident that damaged his spine, and had to take two years off work to recuperate. This accident and Tony's long convalescence were a challenge for our relationship in many ways. For one thing, sex was out of the question because the discs in Tony's spine were pressing on his nerves, and he needed surgery. He had to avoid most physical activity until the surgery was carried out and he had made a complete recovery. I cared for him during his convalescence, and going through such a serious illness together made us closer than ever. Without Tony, and without the various friends and acquaintances who had offered me support over the years, I could have ended up in the same situation as Mum and Daniel. Caring for Tony during his convalescence was, I felt, the least I could do for someone who had transformed my life.

As my relationship with Tony became ever more stable and serious, I looked back and realised that he had saved me from an awful future, and that despite my efforts to work and do well, I could still easily have gone down the wrong path. Given all that had happened in my past, our financial troubles as a family, and my vulnerability as a young man, it would have been easy for me to slip into prostitution, or to succumb completely to my OCD – which was still something that I was learning to overcome. Gradually, I started to understand that it was difficult for me to recognise when I was in a dangerous situation, because I had been in a dangerous situation the whole time when I was growing up, and it seemed perfectly ordinary, because it was all I knew. Living with violence and alcoholism was normal for me. I had also grown up finding it quite difficult to understand the difference between abusive and loving behaviour. Because my grandfather had been kind to me in many ways, I had not been able to identify his molestation of me as a young teen as abusive, and I had blamed myself for everything. Because Tony had high expectations for me, and treated me like an intelligent, responsible person, I began to respect myself and to recognise myself in his understanding of who I was. Because he refused to entertain my OCD and demanded that I push myself to behave normally, I finally started getting a sense of control over it. I began to understand that I had been terribly damaged by my abusive childhood – and that I did not have to let that damage and abuse define who I am forever, but could give myself permission to start getting better. As Tony and I grew closer, I realised that I could talk to him about everything, and that he would never blame me for the awful things that had happened. I understood that, probably for the first time in my life, I was truly loved.

***

In 2003, Crimewatch announced that the police had managed to sequence the DNA in the sperm left on Lesley Molseed's undergarments and that they now had fresh hope that they would be able to find her killer, all these years later. Once again, everyone in the local area was talking about the crime and the fact that the killer might still be around, almost thirty years on. Once again, the local newspapers reported on the story in lavish detail, with plenty of speculation. If the murderer had been a young man when Lesley Molseed was killed, he might still be middle-aged, and girls and women might still be at risk from him. The police said that if anyone had new information to share, they should come forward and do so, as there was a chance that this cold case could finally be solved.

***

I hadn't seen Dad for a long time when I got a call from the local hospital.

"Your father asked us to let you know that he has been admitted," the voice on the line said. "And to tell you to come up."

"What's wrong with him?"

"If you come to the hospital, we'll be able to share all the details. He has listed you as his next of kin, but we can't really discuss his case on the phone."

Although I didn't care about Dad, I went up to the hospital out of a sense of duty, and with the vague hope that he might be dying.

Dad looked very rough, sitting on the bed and rocking forward and back. Years of lifting boxes, getting drunk, and taking drugs were taking a toll on his health, but he had been admitted because he had taken an overdose and had to have his stomach pumped. He wasn't in any danger, because he had alerted someone almost as soon as he had taken the pills.

"We're having some trouble getting his story straight," the doctor said, tapping a pen against Dad's chart. "Your father claims that he was assaulted by someone at his place of work and that he took the pills afterwards because he was in shock and upset. He does have some minor cuts and bruises, but given their superficial nature, their location, and the fact that he took an overdose, we feel that it is most likely that he did it to himself. Can you think of any reason why your father might be self-harming?"

"You'll have to ask him. I don't see him much anymore."

I had the impression that the hospital wasn't taking Dad's suicide attempt that seriously, and I didn't take the account of self-harming very seriously either. Dad had always been much more interested in hurting others than himself, and I was not particularly inclined to be sympathetic.

"He said he had problems with business and that a customer came in and beat him up…"

"I don't know. He always has problems with business, but this is the first I've heard of something like this happening."

"You're the next of kin," the doctor pointed out.

"I hardly ever see my father," I explained. "I really don't know what is going on with him."

"OK," the doctor said. "Well, we'll treat him here, but I am not sure how much we can do for him unless he's straight with us. If there's an underlying issue with his mental health, it would be a good idea to get that looked at. There's not much wrong with him physically."

I went over to Dad in his hospital bed. He looked old and pathetic, even though he was only in his early fifties. I could see some scratches and bruises on his arms, especially his left arm, and noted that they didn't look too bad.

"Can you just do one thing for me?" Dad asked, rocking forward and back in his bed like a child trying to comfort itself.

"What's that?"

"Go up to the house and feed the cats; there's nobody to take care of them. I hate to think of the poor buggers starving because I am in here."

I fed the cats for a week and then Dad was released, having refused the psychiatric support the hospital offered. Maybe he had hoped that I would start visiting him now that he had been sick and in hospital, but I didn't.

I suspected that Dad was anticipating that his pathetic cry for help would persuade Mum to go back to him and in fact, as soon as he got out he was on the phone to her, inviting her over for tea and encouraging her to stay and chat when she brought Daniel around to play video games. I was proud of Mum for having the courage to refuse, and for standing up for herself for once. She told him in no uncertain terms that their marriage was over, and that she would never go back to him.

***

Not long after Dad's brief stay in hospital, Mum phoned me to share some interesting news.

"You'll *never* guess what I just saw in the local paper," she said.

"Go on then, what is it?"

It turned out that Dad had got married, and he had put a wedding announcement in the paper to let the world know. Karen and he had met on a dating website. Some years younger than Mum, Karen had a strong physical likeness to her and a few kids of her own, from a series of failed relationships. Dad had told Karen a string of lies to persuade her that he was a good catch, when the reality was that he was bankrupt. He said that he was a former Marine, which was why he had a bad back. Karen was inclined to believe him, because she was so vulnerable and she desperately wanted to feel a sense of hope about her life. All of her children were from different fathers, most of whom had been abusive towards her, and none of whom helped her with their kids. She thought that she had met someone who cared for her and who would offer her and her children a safe family home.

Now that Dad had a new family to support, he kept the whole show on the road by selling off his stock on the Internet little by little, letting the mortgage go into arrears, and refusing to communicate with the bank. We heard snippets about their lives because Jason's children – Jason had married and started a family, but had grown apart from the rest of the family – went to school with Karen's and he often bumped into Dad at the school gates, and because Dad still insisted on Daniel visiting him during the week to play videogames. At one point, Jason and Dad had got into a fight and Dad had called the police, although he didn't pursue it.

***

One day in 2005, Tony asked me if I wanted to go the gym and, when we had finished working out, we got into the same jacuzzi where we had met.

"Nick," Tony said. "There is something I want to ask you."

"What is it?"

"Would you like to get married?"

There are no words to describe how I felt in that moment. What could I say? The answer could only be "yes", a thousand times over.

There was no same-sex marriage in Britain then, but in 2006 we had a civil partnership ceremony attended by Tony's family – who had welcomed me with open arms since I moved in with him – and our closest friends. I was so happy, I felt as though I was floating on air. The only thing I regretted was not having my mother and brother at the ceremony, but I also knew that I had done the right – in fact the only possible – thing in reducing our contact until they were in a better place and could respect my boundaries. I changed my surname to Tony's, and had no intention of letting my family's shit ever drag me down again. From now on, I would be my own man and Tony's beloved. While I was not legally allowed to refer to Tony as my husband, that is what he was. I did not expect ever to see my father again, and tried not to even think about him. This was a new chapter – in fact, it was a whole new book. This was my life now, and it was wonderful.

***

When the police knocked on my door that morning after Bonfire Night and told me that Dad had been arrested and accused of the murder of little Lesley Molseed, I collapsed. Apart from the horror of hearing what he had done, I felt as though my dreams of a happy life, undogged by my father and his violence and abuse, might be ripped away from me at any moment. I noted that I was not even remotely surprised to hear that Dad had killed a little girl, and I was even less surprised when I learned that he also had a record of indecency with minors. I found out that, in 1976, Dad had abducted a little girl and taken her to a derelict house in Rochdale, where he had molested her, and in 1978, he had taken a little boy to a derelict garage and attempted to molest him, but the child had screamed and run away. In the first case, he had been charged, fined twenty-five pounds, and left with a police record. In the second case, Mum had actually gone to court to support him and provide an image of the loving wife at home, showing that Dad had made a silly mistake, but was not really dangerous because he was a family man with a young wife and child who loved him and needed him. Dad was fined twenty-five pounds again, and that was it; a small price to pay for what he had done. Dad had murdered Lesley while Mum was in hospital, recovering from complications after giving birth to Jason. It was all utterly horrifying.

Now, thanks to the prostitute who had accused him of rape, the police had got Dad on DNA evidence, and it looked as though the family of Lesley Molseed was finally going to see the justice that had evaded them for so many years.

I had often wondered why Dad had got married and had children at all. He had clearly despised Mum, and he had always hated Jason and me, having time only for Daniel. Now I understood that he needed us. We were the façade behind which he, a murderer and a paedophile, could hide. With us, he could appear to the world to be a normal family man. With us, he could get away with murder indefinitely – or so he had hoped. Dad had always demanded Mum's gratitude for taking her back after she had an affair with another man and bore his child, but *he* was the one who should have been grateful because, even if she did not realise it, her presence in his life had kept him safe from close investigation by the police.

***

With Dad arrested, the legal machine kicked into action. Our family was assigned a family liaison officer, who saw each of us separately, and asked me if I wanted to see Mum.

"The next little while is going to be tough for all of you," she said gently. "It will be easier if you can confront it together."

Although I had not been in the same room as Mum for three years, I realised that this was something we needed to face as a united front. Our first meeting after all that time was in the presence of the police and, given the enormity of what was happening to our family, we both chose not to address our estrangement or revisit any of the harsh words that had been exchanged. We had bigger things to deal with now.

"Nicky," Mum said when she saw me. "I am so sorry. I had no idea."

Mum told me that she had gone to court to support Dad back in the seventies, but that she had had no idea that he had been accused of molesting children. If she had, she would not have stayed with him, and Daniel and I would never have been born.

"I knew he wasn't right," she said now, "but I was sure that you boys were safe because I knew that he likes girls, not boys. I thought that I could cope with him and keep you safe. I thought that if I did what he wanted, that might be enough."

I gave Mum the benefit of the doubt, but I have often wondered how she could stay with a man whom she knew liked children of either gender. Ultimately, I suppose, she had no financial independence and felt that she had few, if any, choices. She genuinely believed that he offered her the best possible chance of a good life.

Knowing what I did now about my father and his predilections, I had to wonder if he had ever done anything to hurt Daniel. Daniel had been a beautiful child, with huge blue eyes and flaxen hair, and while Dad had been hard on all of us as children, there had been times when he doted on his youngest. Sometimes, when he and Mum were fighting, Dad would say, "Well, if you fuck off, you can take Jason and Nick with you, but there's no way in hell I am letting you have Daniel." While Mum had always tried never to leave Jason and me alone with Dad, because she knew that he found us irritating and that he might lash out and hurt us, she had felt confident leaving Daniel with him because he was fond of him and she felt sure he wouldn't hurt him badly. I wondered if Daniel's emotional health issues had been caused by Dad abusing him, but Daniel wasn't saying anything.

Now that the police had DNA evidence, it was easy to look at Dad's other crimes towards young children and figure out what happened with Lesley. Presumably he abducted her as he had abducted the others, and ordered her to touch him inappropriately. She must have screamed and threatened to tell and, panicked at the thought of getting into trouble, he had stabbed her frail body until she died. Of course, the fact that he had a weapon with him suggests that he must always have known that her death was a possibility, that the other children are lucky to have survived their encounters with him, and that it is possible that he may have more victims whose remains have not been found.

Back in the 1970s, the police didn't take DNA samples because the technology wasn't there to process them, but they had retained the physical evidence from the case and now they were able to retrieve DNA from a piece of Sellotape that had been used to lift dried semen from Lesley's undergarments. Dad had been lucky for years, and it was bitterly ironic that his habit of visiting prostitutes had been the thing that finally tripped him up. We learned that he had been in his early twenties when he killed Lesley, and had attended a psychiatrist for a period after that. I wondered what had driven him to molest those children and kill Lesley, and why – and if – he had stopped. I remembered the story about how Dad had been beaten badly by the police after his involvement in a robbery. Had they been harsh with him because they knew, or suspected, that he was capable of so much more? Had they been hoping that, if they roughed him up, he might confess to a lot more than theft?

I never met the woman whose accusation of rape was the final piece of the puzzle but, as a victim of rape myself, I could appreciate how brave she had been. Working as a prostitute, it took courage to go to the police. Sex workers are not always treated with respect, and their evidence can be dismissed because of the type of work they do, and because they are often emotionally frail and vulnerable. The rape charges were not pursued in her case because of her mental instability, but if she had not reported my father for what he did to her, he would never have been charged. This woman, whose name was never released to the public for obvious reasons, was instrumental in bringing Dad to justice, and her bravery in reporting her rape should be commended.

Mum and I met Karen, Dad's second wife. We visited her in our old family home, which was now under armed guard in case anyone decided to torch it while Karen was there with her children. Karen was devastated to find out that the man that she had married was a murderer and a paedophile, and she was struggling to come to terms with the change in her circumstances. At first, she had refused to believe anything the police told her but, as the reality sank in, she was starting to accept it, and to understand that he had needed her so as to appear to the world like a respectable married man.

"The police told me that they are looking at him for other unsolved crimes too," she said, shaking her head. "I can't believe it. How did he get away with it all these years? When I met him, he just seemed to be a normal bloke."

Gradually, it emerged that Dad had told Karen one lie after another. Above all, he had convinced her that he loved her. The reality was that, once the police announced that they had DNA evidence that might lead them to Lesley's killer, Dad had needed another woman to marry him and give the impression that he was a stable family man. After all, it had worked for him before.

It was strange seeing Mum and Karen together. They looked so alike that Karen could have been her younger sister. Even more strangely, they quickly formed a bond over their shared experience and became friends. I liked Karen too, and had nothing but empathy for her. She was a mum with several children, who had always done her best for them with a small income and few resources. The fact that she had chosen Dad to be a partner to her, and a stepfather to her children, spoke reams about the limited options in her life.

***

From prison, Dad wrote letter after letter to the press, insisting that he was being stitched up and that he was not guilty of anything. He wrote countless letters to Mum, asking her to support him in court, as she had all those years before. With her help, he felt that he would be able to get off and resume his life as before. It made me sick to know that, if Dad had never murdered Lesley, he would have had no need to marry Mum, and that my very existence in the world is an outcome of his awful crime.

While I was trying to avoid seeing the blaring headlines in the newspaper, to avoid the press, and to evade questions from curious acquaintances, there was absolutely no doubt in my mind that Dad was guilty. I just hoped that the jury would see things the same way.

Chapter Seven: The Trial

Finally, the big day had arrived; the day of my father's trial. It had been a very long time coming. Dad had been arrested on the fifth of November, 2006, had pleaded not guilty on the nineteenth of April, 2007, and had his bail refused on the twenty-third of the same month. We had been told that the trial would start in July but, because Dad's legal team had not been ready, they had asked for a delay. They said that they had not got their evidence ready, but the reality was that they had no evidence and were just stalling for time. Finally, a date was set; the twenty-second of October. Although clearly Dad knew that he had been arrested because of the DNA left on Lesley's body, he was confident that he would not be found guilty and, I believe, had even managed to convince himself that he had not killed Lesley. He had been in prison all this time and, I am sure, was eager to get out. Child killers do not have an easy time in jail, where even the inmates have their standards, and paedophiles and child murderers are seen as the lowest of the low.

The twelve months I spent waiting for my father to face the court had been the longest year of my life. In the decade since Mum and I had finally gathered together the courage to leave him, I had managed to build a life for myself, and thought that I had largely recovered from my childhood. After moving in with Tony and learning how to defend my boundaries, I had achieved real happiness. Now I discovered that the fear, pain, and self-loathing that had been with me every day while I was growing up had just been buried all this time. They had returned, and with a vengeance. All the demons I had buried away for years were back out again, and I would have to start dealing with everything that I had chosen to ignore. I knew with absolute conviction that Dad was guilty, but I was afraid that he would get off. Worse yet, the police had told me that I would have to give evidence when the prosecution tried to paint a picture of his character and typical behaviour. Since hearing that, I had found it impossible to sleep through the night. My weight had plummeted and my eyes were permanently red and swollen. Every day, I struggled through work and came home to Tony, who had to deal with me crying and spewing out a lifetime's worth of secrets. I was dreading giving evidence and could not quite believe that it was really going to happen. I was afraid that maybe Tony was beginning to realise that I wasn't worth the effort; that maybe I wasn't good enough for him, after all. A number of people whom I had considered to be good friends of ours dumped us unceremoniously when they learned that I was the son of a killer. They crossed the road to avoid me when we met in the street. Tony had not yet been out as a gay man at work, and now that the case was in the media, he had to tell his bosses about me and our relationship. Thankfully, they were supportive, and assured him that his sexuality and his relationship with me would not cause him any problems at work.

"You'll be fine on the day," Tony kept reassuring me. "It won't be as bad as you think."

But I had never been in a courtroom before, and all I knew about giving evidence had been learned from watching legal dramas on TV. Usually, it seemed that the witness was shouted at by a series of red-faced barristers while they cringed and shrank in their chair. I didn't think I knew anything relevant to the murder, which had taken place several years before I was even born... but what if I did, and didn't know it? What if I gave evidence against Dad, but he didn't get convicted, and held a grudge against me? What if I answered a question the wrong way, and somehow it got Dad off? I knew what he was capable of. What if I unwittingly told an untruth? Would I get done for perjury? Every time I went to bed at night, these thoughts tormented me. And then there was the press; they would be all over this case, trying to figure out the motivations of the monster who had killed the little girl, all those years ago. I could already imagine the headlines: *House of Horrors; Face of Evil*. Would they tar all of Dad's family with the same brush? Would people assume that his sordid behaviour – the prostitutes, the domestic violence, the leering, and the pawing at young girls – were common to the whole family? That I also had a taste for children, just because I was his son? I could already imagine leaving the courtroom every day and having to make my way through a forest of journalists pointing their cameras and yelling their questions at Mum and me.

We had been assigned a family liaison officer who was kind and helpful. Linda had been through this a thousand times before, she told us. She would lead us through every step of the way and, although it would be difficult, we would come through it and we would be all right.

"You'll be OK," she said. "People will understand that it's not your fault. There'll always be those few who say horrible things, but all you can do is hold your head high and accept that you can't do anything to stop them. It will come to an end, and then you can get on with the rest of your lives."

Mum and I were taken on a secret visit to Bradford Court to see where we would have to stand in the witness box, and where we could go if we needed to take a break. Linda told us that the trial would be easier to bear if we knew what we were going to have to deal with, and where we would be as Dad faced the judge and jury.

"Don't worry about the press," Linda said reassuringly. "We will be able to sneak you in and out so that they don't bother you. We know that it's going to be hard enough for you without going through that. Relax; it won't be as bad as you expect."

I appreciated the thought, but didn't believe her.

Tony was worried about me, and all the stress was taking an inevitable toll on our relationship. He was working hard, and then coming home and having to be there for me, listening to me saying the same things about my fears and anxieties over and over again. I didn't want to go out and socialise because I hated the fact that our friends knew what I was going through and what a rotten, sick family situation I had grown up in. Feeling worthless and ashamed, I had little interest in physical intimacy – I didn't feel that I deserved affection. I became increasingly tense as the trial date grew close, and I knew that it was having an impact on Tony and on our relationship.

"We've got to get away," Tony said. "Even if it's just for a little while. We need to spend at least some time without this hanging over us constantly."

There was a constant stream of press reports, and I was sure that every time I walked down the street there were people sniggering and laughing at me behind their hands. My bosses were not supportive. They gave me just two days of compassionate leave. My doctor gave me a certificate to take some time off work because of stress. Tony and I booked a one-week holiday in Turkey just to escape from the madness for a few days. On holiday, I was never able to completely forget what lay ahead, but at least I knew that the people we passed had no idea who I was. Tony was right; it did help a little.

In early October, two weeks before the trial was due to begin, I was told that I would not be called to testify after all; the statement that I had already given the police would do, because it provided a clear picture of Dad's character. In my statement, I had summarised what it had been like growing up with Dad, describing his violence, how he had humiliated Mum, and how he had destroyed his children's childhoods. The police had asked me questions about his cars and how many cars he had had access to, if he had been sexually or physically abusive, and if I felt that he was guilty of the crime he had been accused of. I had answered as truthfully as I could, given that the crime he was accused of had taken place several years before I was born.

Mum was a key witness in the trial, as she knew better than anyone how brutal Dad could be, and she had already been with him at the time of Lesley's murder. I knew that giving her evidence before the court was going to be terribly difficult for her because she was still afraid of him, and because it meant accepting that she had made some very bad decisions in her life. Ten years ago, she had finally found the strength to leave my father and all the abuse he had meted out to her. Now, she feared she would have to stand up in court and, beneath that awful stare of his, the one that he had always used to silence her, give her testimony.

I realised that as I was off the hook, I would have to be strong for Mum. I had sworn to build some distance between us, but these were not ordinary circumstances, and now I needed to be there for her. While we had not been close for a number of years, the immediacy of the trial brought us together, at least for now. Thankfully, she was given permission to give her evidence via video-link so that she did not have to be in the same room as the man who had made her life hell for so long.

I was given eight weeks' leave from work to attend Dad's case. I felt that it was essential for me to be there, to see justice being done, and to support my mother. The first two days passed slowly, with legal wrangling and the jury being sworn in. Mum's evidence was to be given on the 24th, and I had to stay with her until then. That meant that I could not go into the court room until after that day.

We were driven to the back of the court building in a specially designated people carrier. Mum huddled down on the back seat, covered up so that the press and the angry crowds couldn't see her. Women in her situation are often assumed to be at least somewhat guilty by association. "She must have known," people say. "She must have known all that time and never said anything." Mum was right to be worried, and in fact a number of people in our home town had already come up to her and asked her if she had known that Dad was a killer and if she had been covering up for him for years. While she had not had close friends, many of the people who had been happy to have a chat with her before now wanted nothing to do with her, and she had become even more isolated. She feared that people were talking about her behind her back, saying that she must have been hiding evidence of her husband's crimes all this time. The sad truth is that they probably were.

We were rushed in through the judge's entrance, and brought upstairs in a small, shiny elevator, followed by a steep flight of stairs. As it was not clear what time Mum would be called, we were shown into a waiting room. We had been prepared for a long wait, so we had books and magazines that we browsed through, although neither of us could focus on the contents. There was a television, so we tried watching a film, although of course day time chat shows or a news channel were out of the question, because we couldn't know what was being said about the case. After what seemed like an eternity, a court official came in, coughed, and told Mum that they were ready for her.

Mum was calm as she was led away – *too* calm, I thought. I had been so stressed and worried about giving evidence when it seemed that I would have to. How was she managing not to break down? I got up and paced the room, trying to control my breathing and stay calm.

What will happen to her, I thought, *if she crumbles? Will her blood pressure go up? Will she faint? Will she burst into tears? Will her testimony be considered reliable? Will he somehow find some way of getting to her even though she is in a different room?*

After an hour, Mum was brought back to the waiting room. I explored her face for signs of stress. She looked OK. She must have managed to find the strength to go through with it.

"How are you?" I asked. "Was it OK?"

"I'm all right," she said, a little distantly. "I'm here, aren't I? I got through it. Did what I had to do. At least it's over now."

Mum sat down and ate the lunch that had been brought for her in her absence, and then made her way to the ladies' room to wash her face, saying that she needed to cool down.

The door opened and our family liaison officer came in, accompanied by two police officers, one of whom introduced himself as Max McLean, the officer in charge of the case. This was the man who had worked so hard to bring Dad to justice and to right the many police errors that had seen Stefan Kiszko sent to jail thirty years earlier.

"How do you do?" said Max. He had a posh accent, I noted, and kind eyes that did not seem to be judging us. Max turned to Mum, who had just re-entered the room.

"I just wanted to thank you," he said, "for giving your evidence. I know that it must have been painfully difficult for you, and I want you to be aware that you should be proud of yourself for holding it all together in the face of so much stress. If it wasn't for you and your courage, it would be much harder to build a case against your ex-husband."

Max didn't look at me and, in fact, seemed very reluctant to have any eye contact.

I wonder why he won't look at me, I thought, a knot of paranoia rising in my throat. *Does he think I'm like my father? Maybe I disgust him.* Then I calmed myself: *It's OK,* I thought. *He's just being sensitive. He doesn't know how I might react. After all, this is all about my dad and the things he is being tried for.*

I wanted to speak to Max, to tell him that it was all right, that I understood that the court case was all about justice being done, and that nobody wanted my father to receive the punishment he deserved more than I did. But I couldn't find the words. I couldn't speak at all.

Max left, and Linda and the remaining officer sat down.

"I'd like to introduce you to Robert," Linda said. "Robert is the family liaison officer for the victim's family. For the Molseeds."

I looked at Robert. He was an older, grandfatherly man with a stocky build, glasses and greying hair. He had a kind face and he smiled at me reassuringly.

But what's he doing here? I wondered. *What's he got to do with us?*

"Nick, Beverly," Linda said. "We have a question for you. Would you like to meet Lesley's family? They have expressed an interest in meeting you. Now, you don't have to do anything you don't feel comfortable with…"

I had been standing, and now I sat down. I felt cold suddenly, although at the same time I could feel sweat breaking out on my forehead.

My God, I thought. *They blame us. They think that I am a monster like my father. Maybe they want to beat me up.*

My heart was beating so heavily, it seemed as though everyone else should be able to hear it.

"What do they want to meet us for?" Mum asked in a small voice. "None of it is our fault. We didn't do anything."

Linda seemed to understand our fears straight away.

"Don't worry," she said. "They just want a little chat; they feel they need some clarity. It's all part of the grieving process. They're going through a lot of difficult emotions right now. They're so happy that it seems that Lesley will have justice at last, but the case has brought a lot of the hurt and pain back, too. They've been through an awful lot over the years, and this is bringing it all back to them."

Mum and I looked at each other. We didn't have to speak.

"That's fine," Mum said. "Of course, we can meet them."

"We'll both stay with you all the whole time," Robert assured us. "You will never be alone with them and there is nothing to be afraid of. I've got to know them quite well, and they are very nice people."

Linda looked at her watch.

"The court is breaking for lunch now," she said, "so while that's happening, we can move you to a bigger, more comfortable room in the court area."

Outside, we were joined by a woman whose job it was to make things in the courthouse go as smoothly as possible. The smartly dressed lady with soft grey hair gave us a friendly smile. I noticed that she was wearing a lavender perfume. Discreetly, I inhaled the relaxing scent.

Mum and I followed Linda and the lavender lady, whose name we were not given, down a long, winding corridor, our footsteps hushed by the thick blue carpet on the floor. The walls of the corridor were pierced here and there by large, imposing beech doors. Each one bore a gold plaque stating the name and purpose of the room. Many were dedicated to police activities, and there was one that was pointed out to us.

"You must never, *ever*, approach this area," Linda said severely. "These are the judge's quarters. When you are walking in this area, you must remain completely quiet."

Feeling intimidated, Mum and I nodded to show that we understood and that we would do our best to never do anything that might disturb one of the judges.

Eventually, we reached a side room that had double doors onto the main corridor, and was shielded with blinds from the chaos of the court rooms. I was relieved to see the blinds, as I knew that neither of us would cope if we were bombarded by journalists and other curious people. The lavender-scented lady showed us around. There were two toilets, and facilities for making tea and coffee. The high, vaulted ceiling had fancy cornicing, the floor was carpeted in dark blue, and some similarly coloured sofas furnished the waiting area.

"This is the old part of the building," the lavender lady explained, indicating the architectural flourishes. "The whole place is a mishmash of old and new. Anyway, hopefully you have everything you need to make yourselves comfortable."

"Are you nearly ready to meet Lesley's family?" Linda asked.

My heart leapt. Linda indicated a door in a corner of the room that I had not noticed. Mum and I followed Linda across the blue carpet for what felt like an age, and Linda opened the door onto a tiny room stuffed with an orange floral sofa, a television, and a pile of DVDs. A small window provided some natural light.

"You can wait in here," Linda said. "Just settle down and try not to worry too much."

Mum and I went and perched on the sofa.

"All right then," Linda said briskly. "I'll go and have my lunch, and after that we'll have the meeting, OK?"

When Linda had gone, Mum and I looked at the pile of DVDs and chose one to put on. We sat in front of it, neither watching nor listening. I have no memory of that film.

***

Linda opened the door, followed by two women, and then an elderly couple and Robert, the liaison officer. We were about to meet the Molseeds, Lesley's family, here to exact justice after all these years. An overwhelming sensation of horror swept over me. What was going to happen now? I couldn't even look at Mum, let alone try to guess what she was thinking. Somehow, we managed to get to our feet.

The two younger women crossed the room with a couple of steps.

"I'm Laura," one of them said, putting her arms around Mum and hugging her.

"I'm Julie," said the other. She hugged me. This was the last thing that I had been expecting, but it felt right and I let myself relax against her.

Laura told us a little about how my father's crimes had impacted on the whole family. She herself had been in therapy for years because of what had happened to Lesley. We assured her that we had never known a thing. They thanked us for testifying against Dad, saying that they could only imagine how hard it must have been for us.

The hour or so that followed passed in what seemed like an instant. Lesley's father, imposing in a suit, spoke with a thick Glasgow accent. April, her mother, was buxom and down-to-earth. Lesley's sisters were petite and smartly dressed. Perhaps Lesley would have looked like them if she had lived to grow up. Laura and Julie were warm and friendly, but at the same time somewhat guarded. Well, of course they were.

"There's something we just have to ask," April said to Mum. "Did you ever know what your husband did to our little girl? Did you never suspect that he was the one who had killed her?"

"*No,*" Mum almost shrieked. "If I had, I would have reported him. I would never have let that go. I knew that he wasn't a good man, but I thought that I was the only one he hurt."

"What was he like, your dad?" Julie asked me. "Did *you* have any inkling that he was capable of what he did to our Lesley?"

"Yes," I suddenly found myself saying, "I did. I didn't know that he had killed anyone, but I definitely knew that he was capable of it. I've been afraid of him all my life and, as soon as I had heard what he did, it all made sense."

Suddenly I was telling them about my childhood and the brutality and bullying that we had all suffered at my father's hands. Although they were dealing with their own nightmare, they listened to me with compassion and sympathy.

I remember only a fraction of what was said during that hour. It seemed clear that Laura had been the most badly affected by Lesley's murder. When the meeting was over, April gave a little speech. She said that it had been helpful meeting us, that she hoped we would stay in touch, and that she was sure we could all help each other through this dreadful time.

I was overwhelmed by April's kindness to the family of the man who had extinguished the life of their little girl. After all these years, and everything they had been through – the initial shock, the relief when Stefan Kiszko was found guilty, the horror when it turned out that he had been innocent and had lost sixteen years of his life to prison, and now – finally – the hope that the real killer would be found guilty and put behind bars.

Just before Lesley's family left, her sister Laura gave me a penetrating look.

"Our nightmare is beginning to come to an end," she said. "But yours is just beginning."

By mid-afternoon, I had become enveloped in exhaustion. It had overcome me as my depression had before, destroying all other feeling and make it almost impossible to think rationally about anything. All I wanted was to go home so that I could feel Tony's comforting arms around me and know that I was safe, and that he would never judge me because of my father's actions.

We were driven back to Mum's house, where I had left my car. Mum was tired too, and neither of us spoke much on the way back. We just stared out the windows of the car.

"I can't believe how nice they were," was all Mum said, speaking of Lesley's family. "They didn't blame us at all."

I couldn't believe it either. Although little Lesley had been murdered before I was born, somehow, I felt that we were stained by my father's crimes.

***

Now that Mum had given her evidence, we were both free to go and there was no need for either of us to attend the court proceedings. But I knew that I had to go. I had not been allowed to attend while Mum was giving her testimony, but there was no reason for me not to hear the rest of the case, and both the counsellor I was attending and I felt that it would be a good idea, and that it would help me to achieve a sense of closure and move on with the rest of my life without this awful feeling of guilt hanging over me. I felt that if I didn't see the trial with my own eyes that I would never quite believe it; that it would all seem like a dream, and I would never be completely sure that it was really all about my father.

"I've just got to attend the rest of the hearing," I told Tony. "I'll never be able to let it rest unless I see for myself what happens."

Tony tried to understand why I felt the way I did, but some of our friends thought that I was crazy and that I should just walk away.

"Are you out of your mind?" they asked. "Why put yourself through the ordeal if you don't have to? Just get on with your life and try to forget it."

But I knew that I would never be completely at peace unless I learned for myself what Dad had done. He was my father; I was his son. I needed to be completely sure that I wasn't like him, that I wasn't destined to turn out the way he had. I didn't want to be like any member of the public, relying on newspapers and television to hear the awful, sordid details. I needed to see for myself that he was brought to the dock and made to answer for what he had done – mostly to Lesley, whose young life had been destroyed, but also to everyone else he had hurt and damaged, including Stefan Kiszko, who had served years for a murder that he had not committed. And although I had given a statement and Mum had testified against him, until I saw Dad in the courtroom with my own eyes, I wouldn't quite believe that it was all real. Despite everything, until the moment I learned that Dad had murdered an innocent child, a small part of me had respected him and wanted him to love me. That part had died. I didn't know what would take its place.

"If you have to go, I'll support you," Tony said. "But I don't think you should go on your own."

Tony's stepmother agreed. She and I had become very close since Tony and I got together, and

Anne said that she would accompany me every day so that I did not go through the trial on my own.

While he was supportive of my decision to attend the trial, Tony was also very worried about my mental health. He could see what a toll the trial was having on my emotional well-being, and was concerned that it could lead to a breakdown.

"Look," he said one night as we lay in bed. "Are you sure you are strong enough for this? Nobody will think any less of you if you change your mind."

"I just have to do it," I insisted. "It would be so much worse not knowing what is going on."

"OK. I don't understand why, but I'll be here when you get home. I'll pick up the pieces when it makes you ill, because I know it will, and I will be your shoulder to cry on when you need it."

I just turned around and hugged him.

Because Tony is a police officer, he had to be careful not to get too involved in the case. We were both concerned that my father's case would somehow have negative repercussions for his career, and I worried in my darkest moments that Tony would leave me because he did not want to be associated with the son of a murderer, and risk everything that he had worked for. Never having met my father, all he wanted was to provide us with a safe home and know that our lives would not be touched by the misery and devastation in my past. I wished that I could promise him that they wouldn't.

Anne and I agreed to share the driving throughout the trial. I knew that there would be days when I was too drained to face it. Anne had worked in courts and knew how everything was organised. The first day, she parked in the outside car park, adjacent to the court building. We got out of the car, and she squeezed my hand as we turned to walk towards the door.

"You'll be fine," Anne said.

I felt a lot less certain.

We walked around the corner and I felt my legs buckle as I saw rows of news vans and hordes of photographers pointing enormous cameras at everyone going into the building. I hadn't realised it, but photographers take pictures of everyone going in and out, relying on getting identifications for them later.

"Stay strong," Anne whispered, as she slipped her arm through mine. "They don't know who you are."

We walked past the photographers and news vans, through the metal detectors at the entrance, and into the relative safety of the court house.

The court house had various rooms. Dad's trial was being held in room eleven. As Anne and I approached, I saw Linda hovering outside a police room. She came over to ask how I was, and introduced herself to Anne. Having already been through several days of court, she had some useful advice.

"Go and have a drink and go to the loo now," Linda said. "There aren't many breaks."

"Come on; you can come into our room," she said, when we had acted on her suggestion.

Linda brought Anne and me into a room packed with members of Lesley Molseed's family: sisters, aunts and uncles, cousins. They had all been waiting for over thirty years for justice to be done. At least ten of them turned up every single day for the trial.

The next few days followed the same pattern. Anne and I came to listen to the devastating evidence being given against my father, and were taken care of by Lesley's large, warm family.

I wore a suit to the trial each day.

"Aren't you smart?" Linda teased. "Look; your socks match and all."

My matching socks and shirt became a running joke.

Coming from a family unit that had never been close, I was overwhelmed by all the love and support the Molseed family showed me, and started to feel as though I was being suffocated. Day after day, the lies and brutality that had formed my childhood and ended Lesley's were being wrenched from my father and the various witnesses, and yet here I was, held in the collective embrace of the family that had lost so much. None of it made any sense. Anne understood what I was feeling, and explained to Linda that I needed a little space. We withdrew somewhat, but I was still aware of the love and care coming from the Molseeds every time one of them caught my eye as we all sat in the public gallery.

I sat each day in the same seat, in the second row back, right against the glass screen, through which I could look at my father. I wanted him to see me and the grief and pain that must have been etched clearly on my face. I wanted him to know how much I despised him, and that from now on I disowned him completely and would have nothing to do with him. Dad would not look over and give me the eye contact I craved. He knew I was there, because he must have seen me when we had to stand each time the judge entered and left the courtroom. I wasn't sure until, one day, a security guard escorted him to the witness stand and right past where I was sitting. Everyone watched as Dad walked around the public gallery. He dropped his head as he went past the Molseeds and then me.

As the trial took place, a picture of Lesley emerged. She had been a little slow and very trusting, not very strong, with poor health as she had been born with a hole in her heart. She had also been a happy little girl known to her family as a chatterbox, who was always willing to help, and who was loved by everyone. I realised that Lesley had been the start of a pattern in which Dad targeted girls and women who were easy to manipulate. We heard that the second girl Dad abducted also had a learning disability; the police had been able to track her down and interview her, and her testimony was used in the case against him. Mum, while of normal intelligence, had suffered from low self-esteem all her life. All the girls and women whose lives Dad had blighted had lived with multiple problems of their own. They had been easy targets for a man like him.

October became November. Anne and I continued to attend court, while at home my behaviour became erratic as my old demons returned to haunt me. I started once again to display the characteristic symptoms of Obsessive Compulsive Disorder. Tony was desperately worried, although he did not try to convince me to stop attending the trial. He made a point of arranging outings for us at the weekends and encouraged me not to buy newspapers or watch television so that I could take my mind off the trial, and so that our home could remain a safe haven, to which I could retreat in the evenings.

"You've got to switch off from it when you're not there," he insisted. "You've got to have some release. Don't let it follow you home."

I tried to take Tony's advice, but didn't always manage it. I did pick up a paper now and again and, inevitably, the case was covered in excruciating, but not always accurate, detail. One story maintained that Dad had earned about £50,000 a year selling comics and that we had been a comfortably-off family. That had been far from the truth. Dad had always been in debt, the house remortgaged to the hilt and falling into disrepair, the cars bought on hire purchase, and his wife and children walking around in rags. That was true for us, and it was also the case in his second marriage to Karen. He had never been a good provider. There had been days when there was not enough to eat. Even before I knew about Lesley, I had resented him for having failed as a father and not having cared for us as a parent should.

I was attending therapy, and I think that this helped me to stay relatively sane. The simple fact of being able to unload my thoughts and feelings onto someone who didn't know me personally made all the difference. But then I would return to the courtroom, and as I sat and listened to the many witnesses giving their evidence, I felt as though my life was flashing before me on a film reel. I saw Dad pushing Mum down the stairs. I saw him beating Jason up. I saw him taunting me and waving his guns around. I heard the ugly words he used to make fun of me because he thought that I was effeminate. From a third-person perspective, I saw myself burying my head under my pillow as Mum cried out because Dad was raping her yet again.

I looked at Dad on the witness stand and wondered how he had messed up so royally. Dad had come from a well-to-do family and he had been given every chance in life. He had been spoilt as a child by his accountant father and his mother, who had an allowance from her affluent father, had been given a private education and piano lessons, and had been told that he wasn't common like other people, but something special. Grandma had often told me about how she, Grandad and Dad had been invited to parliament functions because of their fundraising and canvassing to get Cyril Smith into parliament. I reasoned that my grandparents had probably used their money and local influence to get Dad out of trouble every time he did something wrong. Dad had been given every reason to succeed, but look at the life he had created for himself. He had failed at everything he had ever done, betrayed everyone who ever loved him, and now he was on trial for murder.

Dad sat in the dock with his glasses on the end of his nose, passing notes to his barrister, and grinning as though he were enjoying all the attention. The junior barrister was a young woman, and Dad, at fifty-five bald and seriously overweight, was even trying to flirt with her, in full view of everyone in the court room. It was grotesque. Did he seriously believe that, aged fifty-five, overweight and bald and – above all – on trial for the murder of a child, she might be interested in him? It was also obvious that Dad was so delusional that, somehow, he had managed to convince himself that he really hadn't killed Lesley, just as he was sure he had not hurt the other children he had molested. He probably believed that he had been a good husband and father, too.

One day, I noticed a woman in the press gallery who looked very familiar. Finally, I realised who she was: Nichola McAuliffe, who had played Sheila Sabatini in the TV show *Surgical Spirits*. Nichola approached the Molseeds and chatted with them, and then Anne and I were introduced to her. She explained that she was working as a journalist and was writing a piece for *The Guardian* about the case. I was wary about speaking to a journalist, but Nichola was kind.

"You're being very brave, coping with everything so well," she said. "I know it's not easy."

Anne and I were touched that Nichola had gone out of her way to talk to us, and that she had been so understanding. I was still wary of journalists, but I realised that not all of them were out to twist someone's words until they said something very different to what they had intended.

Eventually, the forensic scientist was called to give evidence. There was some squabbling about her qualifications and suggestions that the evidence had been contaminated, and the day ended up getting cut short, with the expert being asked to return the following morning.

Bloody hell, I thought as we drove home. *What if he gets off on some sort of technicality?*

I was very disturbed by the thought that the jury might be swayed by all the talk about contamination. Faced with the possibility that Dad would get off, I began to think that maybe the best thing I could do would be to end my life. After dropping Anne off at her house, I could put my foot on the accelerator and drive off a motorway bridge, or tell Tony that I was taking the dogs for a walk and then step in front of a lorry. What was worse; the thought of Dad getting off, or knowing that the world knew him as a murderer and serial paedophile? Maybe there was something wrong with me that hadn't shown up yet. Maybe the world would just be a better place without me.

The phone rang. It was Linda, who instinctively knew that I must be worrying.

"I know you're concerned about what happened in court today, but I want you to know that it's all OK," she said. "This is perfectly normal. Your father's lawyers are just doing their job and contesting anything that puts him in a bad light. We've been told to expect them to claim that there was cross-contamination, but we know the evidence is sound. The British justice system guarantees a proper defence to everyone, and your father is as entitled to it as anyone else – but getting a good defence does not mean that he'll get off."

The next day, the scientist was given the chance to finish her testimony, and she did a fantastic job. As she stepped down from the witness stand, everyone in the court room knew that Dad's barristers' attempts to quash the physical evidence had failed.

Now there was only one person left to speak: Ronald Castree. My father. Dad. This was the moment that we had all been waiting for.

Dad heaved his overweight body up in the stand and swore to tell the truth, the whole truth, and nothing but the truth. He was wearing the same outfit that he had had on throughout the trial; a pale grey suit with a white shirt and black tie. He towered over his barrister, a tiny man with a thin face dominated by a pair of glasses. I had seen the barrister climbing out of his enormous Mercedes, and wondered how he managed to see over the steering wheel. The diminutive lawyer made Dad look even fatter than ever. Despite the abundant evidence against Dad, the barrister had done a great job of defending him; so good that I was still afraid that, somehow, he would get off.

Dad coughed and loosened his tie. He had put on so much weight in jail that he no longer had any neck to speak of. He gave his barrister his story, and then was cross-examined by a lawyer called Mr Goose, who was a tall man with dark hair and an imposing presence. Mr Goose's voice boomed across the room as he began to question Dad about his version of events.

I suddenly found that I was shaking. I gripped Anne's hand and squeezed it very hard.

Shit, I thought. *Somehow, he's going to manage to convince the jury that he couldn't possibly have committed this heinous crime.*

Dad explained in detail how he had always worked very hard to support his wife and provide for "the lad", by which he meant my brother Jason. He presented himself as an excellent husband and father except for one little thing.

"I'll not tell a lie," he said. "I was not always completely faithful to my wife. On a number of occasions, I had sex on the back seat of my taxi. I believe that Lesley Molseed could have sat in the back of my taxi at some stage and that the semen might have rubbed off onto her garments in this way."

Dad said that all the taxi drivers had sex with the women they picked up in their cabs, and that this was considered perfectly normal behaviour in the 1970s. My father's defence team had already brought up the fact that the social services records showed clearly that Lesley and her sisters regularly went to school in dirty clothing, and may have worn each other's underwear on occasion. This nugget of information was horrible for the Molseed family to hear, especially as they had gone through all of this before.

This can't be real, I thought wildly at one stage. *This is a True Crime show on TV.*

I was snapped back to reality as Dad started to talk about Mum, explaining to the jury how hard he had always had to work to maintain her, as she was a lazy person who sat about at home and refused to do anything, stretching his tolerance to its limit. Without meaning to, I let out a loud tut. Mum's ability to be a good mother had been destroyed by Dad. He had made her life hell, restricting her access to housekeeping money, and blaming her for everything that went wrong in our house. He had belittled her on every possible occasion, until her sense of self was completely destroyed. Everyone turned to look at me, or I thought they did. Anne put her hand on my arm and held it tightly and I managed to prevent myself from crawling across April and the rest of the Molseeds in the front row, running across the court room, and hitting my father as hard as I could.

Dad did his best to convince the jury that he was innocent, but he told so many lies and was so inconsistent that the jury members actually started to shake their heads in disbelief, especially when Dad began to say that he must have had sex with one or more of Lesley's female relatives, suggesting that they were easy women and would have leapt at the chance of sleeping with him, and that the sperm found on the child's clothes must have been transferred from them. The people in the courtroom actually started to laugh out loud when Dad insisted that he could easily have had sex with Lesley's mother and that he would not have remembered, as he had affairs with so many women; apparently the women in the area had found him absolutely irresistible. Dad was sweating uncontrollably by now, his bald head shining under the court room lights. I could see his Adam's apple bob up and down in his throat as he spoke.

I wish the earth would swallow me, I thought. *I can't believe that I am this horrible monster's son.*

I had gone unrecognised so far, but suddenly I was terrified that people might look at me and realise who I was. I had spoken to Nichola McAuliffe, but she obviously hadn't said a word to anyone else. I was never happier to know that I do not resemble my father. I was worried about Mum. She had not attended most of the trial, but now she was waiting upstairs, where she was safe from prying eyes, as she felt that she just had to hear the outcome as quickly as possible.

The summing up and closing speeches were given on the eleventh of November, and the jury went out to reach a verdict while we returned to our sanctuary, the private room that Linda had shown us to on that first day.

"What's going to happen?" I asked the police. "When will they find him guilty?"

"It could still go either way," they said.

I couldn't believe it. After all the damning evidence and Dad's pathetic, rambling attempt to explain himself? Did they really think he might get off?

The jury was out for ages, and it is never a good sign when they take so long to decide. They requested clarification about the DNA evidence, which had suggested that there was just a one in a billion chance that the semen did not belong to Dad, and the scientist in charge had to come back in.

There was no verdict on the eleventh, so on the twelfth we were still alternately sitting and pacing up and down in the private room that our lavender lady kept available for us. By mid-afternoon, we had concluded that nothing was going to happen and that we would have to return the following day when, suddenly, the intercom asked everybody to return to court.

This is it, I thought. *One way or another, it'll all be over soon.*

Mum stayed safely behind closed doors while Anne and I made our way back to the court room in the company of the lavender lady.

"Take deep breaths," Anne told me. "Breathe steadily. Stay grounded, and you will be able to keep calm."

I tried to take her advice, but it took all of my powers of concentration.

In the public gallery, I noticed that a middle-aged woman was sitting in my usual seat. For some reason, this filled me with distress and alarm. I turned to the lavender lady.

"Do you think you could ask her to move for me?" I asked her. She did as I requested.

"Excuse me," the lavender lady said to the woman. "This is the accused's son and he would very much like to sit there. Do you mind?"

It was so quiet in the court room that I knew that everyone must have heard, including the press. My cover was blown.

"Just deal with it," I muttered to myself. "What will be, will be."

I sat down with Anne on my left and the lavender lady beside her. I noticed that Max McLean, the officer in charge of the case, was at the end of my row, sitting with his head bowed over his hands, which were folded in his lap. All the police on the case filed into the room and stood with their backs against the wall. Considering what a mess had been made of the first trial in 1976, I am sure that they needed to hear justice being done at last. The case against Stefan Kiszko had been a blot on the reputation of the local police force ever since.

Anne and I gripped each other's hands so tightly they turned white. The foreperson of the jury, a woman with dark hair, stood up and cleared her throat. I looked at her, back down at my feet, and then at Max McLean. I could not look at my father.

"We find the defendant guilty," she said, explaining that only two members of the jury had disagreed with this verdict.

The judge announced that there would be a short break before sentencing. As soon as we were allowed to stand, the lavender lady took me by the hand and rushed me through the corridors to where Mum was waiting to hear the verdict. I felt that I was running as quickly as if a pack of wolves was following me. I just knew that Mum needed to hear the verdict from me and nobody else. After all, she had once loved Dad, however briefly, and she had borne him children. She had lived with him for twenty-three years, during which he slowly extinguished that love with his incessant, degrading abuse. Now she would have to live the rest of her life with the knowledge that the father of her children was a paedophile and a murderer, and that their marriage had been a sham from the start, designed to protect him from suspicion. She had given him her young adult life, and he had turned it into a nightmare.

I pushed open the heavy doors to find Mum inside, alone.

"Guilty!" I shouted. "They found him guilty!"

I started to cry. We met in the middle of the room, our arms around each other for the first time in years. Without letting go, we sank to the floor.

***

As soon as we had pulled ourselves together, Mum phoned Daniel to let him know the verdict and then we sat and waited for me to be called back to the court room. I wondered how long Dad would get. I knew that Stefan Kiszko had served sixteen years for my father's crime, so I hoped that he would serve at least that much. We did not have to wait for long; after a short interval, it was announced that the judge was ready to give the sentence.

Tony's mother, Anne, had driven Mum and me to court.

At least I don't have to drive myself home, I thought. *I'll be able to relax and let it all sink in.*

The judge asked my father to stand to hear his verdict.

"You abducted Lesley Molseed," he said. "You did take her to moor land and sexually assault her and stab her and leave her dying and then returned to your new-born son and family and went out about your life."

Each word the judge spoke seemed to flay another layer from me. With no thought or care as to who could hear and might recognise me, I sobbed loudly. I didn't care about anything anymore. I looked at my father. He was still wearing the same suit and standing in the same position that he had adopted throughout his trial. His glasses had slipped down his face, his arms were folded, and he showed no sign of remorse or of accepting what was happening in the court room. I felt physically ill, nauseated by both my father and myself, the son of a murderer.

"He will serve at least thirty-two years," the judge said.

"Your honour," Dad whined. "I didn't do it."

"Take him down."

I will never forget the sound of the door closing behind Dad as he was led away. I realised that, somehow, he had managed to convince himself that none of it was his fault. Despite the overwhelming evidence against him, he had concocted an absurd story about having sex with Mrs Molseed on the back seat of his taxi, hoping that the stigma attached to the Molseeds' poverty would make the story seem believable. All his young life, Dad's parents had done what it took to keep him out of trouble. Along the way, he had started to think of himself as invincible and untouchable. I wished there was some way of telling his parents that their golden boy was finally going to pay for what he had done.

I went back to the private waiting room and told Mum about the sentence. We both felt that we should leave as soon as possible. I was feeling the overwhelming sensation of just needing to escape, and I knew that there would be hordes of media people outside, waiting to pester us for a statement and to take our photographs for the front page. Thankfully, we were taken out the way we had come in the day Mum gave evidence, and were able to get home in peace.

We would go on to stay in touch with the Molseeds for a while, and even attended a special tree-planting ceremony in memory of little Lesley. It meant a lot to us both that they allowed us to be there.

***

For weeks, I had been useless at home, and an awful partner for Tony. I had not been able to do my share of domestic chores or think about anything but my own and my mother's well-being. Now I knew what I think I had always suspected: my life with my father, the first seventeen years of my life, had been nothing but a lie. I didn't know who or what I was any more.

"Your nightmare is just beginning," Laura Molseed had told me when we met. I was beginning to realise how right she was, and I could only hope that I would have the courage to confront it.

Chapter Eight: Return to Earth

Overwhelmed by how kind the Molseeds were being to the family of the man who had killed their little girl, I had registered Lesley's words when she told me that our nightmare was beginning, but it would take some time before I fully understood. The morning of the verdict, Mum and I had recorded an interview for television with the contact of a journalist friend of mine who worked for Granada. It was going to be broadcast that evening. We both felt strongly about making it clear to the public that we were aghast by what my father had done, and rejected him completely. We also felt that we had done nothing to be ashamed of, and that there was nothing to be gained from hiding ourselves away. Nobody's loss was as great as the Molseeds', but we were victims too. Our family life had never been happy and now we knew that, even on the good days, we had been living with a killer, and that some people would see us as tarnished by his crime. Granada Television was great with us, helping us to express our revulsion and upset, and would go on to win an award for their coverage of the trial. The interview helped to clear the air somewhat, and to clarify to the people we knew that we had never been aware of Dad's crimes.

Throughout the trial, Jason had decided to support Dad and had chosen not to believe that he was guilty. He had not come to the courtroom to attend the trial himself, and he had cut off all contact with Mum, furious with her for agreeing to testify against Dad. Despite the fact that Dad had treated Jason very badly throughout his childhood, and even though Jason now knew that Dad was not his biological father, somehow Dad was still able to control him. Jason had bought into Dad's story of his innocence. All Jason had ever wanted was to be loved by Dad, and apparently that was all he wanted even now.

The last time I spoke to Jason was just after the television interview. Jason was furious.

"If you hadn't testified against him, he would be a free man," he said. "I can't believe you have turned on him like this. Whatever happened to family coming first? Blood being thicker than water? And now you're airing our family business all over the television; he's innocent and he is going to appeal and you are doing your best to spoil his chances."

Although I was pleased that at last the ordeal was over and my father was going to receive the punishment he deserved, I was exhausted and strangely bereft. I had been fixated on the trial from start to finish and, now that it was over, I didn't know how I felt.

"At least it's over," I said to Mum. "We can get back to our normal lives now."

"Thank God," she replied.

I couldn't have been more wrong.

***

The family liaison officer had warned us that there was likely to be considerable media attention focused on us if Dad was convicted.

"My advice is that you give some interviews as soon as possible," she said. "If you don't get your story out in the open, you could end up being hounded. The journalists will try to dig up dirt on you – *any* dirt. And it'll be printed, whether it's true or not. It's much better to give your side of the story straight away and get the media off your backs. If you find a journalist you trust and feel you can talk to, get the interview over and done with."

This reasoning was why we'd recorded the interview with Granada, and why we had agreed to go to London after the verdict for another interview. Reluctantly, we agreed that we would give the journalists what they wanted in the hope that they would leave us alone afterwards.

Anne drove Mum and me back home across the Saddleworth Moors. I looked out at the dull, lonely landscape that I remembered so well from childhood. Every time we'd gone on a family holiday to Centre Parcs, we'd driven through this very area. It had not changed in all these years. I remembered sitting with my face pressed against the glass, watching the moors passing by outside. I would never have guessed how significant that dreary landscape would prove to be for our family in future years. I remembered the holidays vividly; how Dad would spend every moment he could in the pool, surrounded by little girls in their swimsuits. We had thought it was great at the time, but it didn't look like innocent family fun anymore. Even my one happy memory from childhood, of going on holiday, looked dirty and sordid now. Dad had been teaching us how to swim just to have an excuse to get closer to the little girls.

Anne dropped Mum off at her house. Mum needed to make sure that Daniel was OK, and put a few bits and pieces together for the trip to London. Then she brought me home. I went upstairs and opened the door to find Tony having his evening meal in front of the television.

"How was it?" he asked. "Are you OK?"

I shrugged.

"You're on the telly."

Tony reached for the remote control and turned up the volume. The interview that Mum and I had given that morning was being shown. There I was, pouring my heart out to the reporter, with Mum sitting beside me. We looked much more poised and in control than either of us had felt at the time. I sank onto the settee and watched myself on the screen. It didn't seem real. None of it did.

"I wish I could stay," I said to Tony when the interview was over. "I wish I didn't have to go to bloody London."

"I know, love, but it won't be too bad, and it will all be over soon. You've been so strong this long, you can make it."

I put a few things in the bag and returned to the living room for a hug. Tony held me tight.

"Everything is going to be OK," he reassured me. "You'll survive this like you've survived everything. We'll get through it together. All right?"

"All right," I said, my voice muffled against his shoulder. I could not imagine how I would have coped without Tony.

The television studio had arranged for a car to pick up me and then Mum, before bringing us to London. It arrived on time and I climbed inside. Tony waved me goodbye. Then, as soon as the car pulled away from the kerb, Mum rang.

"Jason's been here," she sobbed. "He was in a right old state. He was screaming and swearing at me and he says he's not going to let me see the grandchildren if I go to London to give the interview."

"Mum," I said, trying to reassure her. "He's just upset."

Jason was entitled to his views, and to some extent I could understand his feeling that it was the wrong thing to do, but I was very angry with him for upsetting Mum when she had more than enough to deal with already, and for using his children as pawns. What was wrong with him? Was he still refusing to accept that Dad was guilty?

"That's not all," Mum said. "A lady called Elaine was here from GMTV asking some questions on behalf of the researchers, and he laid into her too."

My heart sank. All Mum and I wanted to do was show the world that we were nice, normal people who had been mistreated by a terrible man. With Jason behaving as he had, who was going to believe that? Maybe they'd think that we were all cut from the same cloth as Dad, after all.

Mum and I were put up in a lovely hotel just behind Westminster, and were interviewed the following morning on GMTV by Fiona Philips and Andrew Castle. They couldn't have been kinder. A few days later, Fiona wrote in her weekend newspaper column that she considered me to be a hero. I had been an abused child and I could have grown up to be violent like my father – but I didn't. A number of television and radio interviews followed, as in the wake of the trial the media was very interested in our family. By early 2008, I was relieved to see that interest in us was fading, and that we could go back to being ordinary, anonymous people.

**

"After all that," I said to Tony, "I feel like it's time to do something different with my life."

"Well, what?"

"I don't know. I just feel that I could offer more than I do now."

Tony and I escaped to Spain for a while, and then we spent weekends at our holiday house in the Lake District. We spent hours and hours talking about what I could do; how I could train for a different profession. I wanted to help people, as I already did, but also to make a difference on a larger scale. I also felt that, although Dad's crimes were not my fault, I had a duty to do something for society, to make reparation for all the damage he had done. After much discussion, together Tony and I decided that I would apply to join the police force. How better to help make Britain a safer place than from the front line?

As a high-ranking officer, Tony had lots of advice.

"Never serve on your own doorstep," he said. "It's not worth the hassle. Apply to work a bit away from home."

I applied to the Greater Manchester Police Force for a position as a Police Community Support Officer. I filled in the form very carefully, feeling extremely positive about my chances. Ever since my father's arrest, I had felt that I was dragging a weight around with me. As I considered the possibility of an exciting new job, doing something that mattered, my spirits rose.

Shortly after I posted off the application, I received a phone call from the recruitment department with a few questions. I answered them and asked if there was any problem.

"We've got to look into your relationship with your father," the recruitment officer explained, "given his criminal past and his conviction."

"I don't understand," I said. "What's that got to do with me? The murder happened before I was born."

"It's just routine."

I hung up and sank into the nearest chair, my head in my hands. Was the police force judging me on the basis of what my father had done? Did they believe in collective guilt, or that the sins of the father are passed on to the son?

A few days later, I received an answer from the police, saying that, following the security checks that had been carried out on my application, they could not offer me a position.

At first, I was angrier than I was upset. Without thinking about it very much, I decided to fight back. I rang my friend Steve Douglas, who works for ITV, and told him what had happened. That very evening, I was on the news again. In the days that followed, there were more television appearances and newspaper articles about my rejection by the police force. I stopped Googling my name because not all the online comments on the articles were kind. I became obsessed with the need to be treated just like anyone else. The people closest to me knew who I was and what I needed to achieve, and that was the main thing.

Tony advised me to lie low for a little while, and promised to speak to his bosses. They in turn suggested that I put together an appeal and send it to the Police Training College in Cheetham Hill. Following this, I was sent an official apology and given a date for interview, provided I ceased discussing the Greater Manchester Police with the press.

Following a very tough interview and examination, I was sent a letter offering me a place in a pool of candidates for when a suitable post came up. Some months later, I was offered a post but, by this point, Tony and I had decided together that I would withdraw my application. I felt that I should have been given an interview based on the merits of my application, and not because the Greater Manchester Police had come under pressure from Police Headquarters, presumably because they feared the publicity that a lawsuit would bring. The whole experience had shown me how often people like me, the children of convicted murderers, face discrimination – not because of anything they've done themselves, but because of their fathers' crimes. I decided that I could use my own experience to advocate for the families of serious criminals. More radio and television interviews followed, as well as a few more appearances in the newspaper and on social media networks. The more I talked, the more I realised that I was very far from alone. I spoke with people from all over Europe and heard their stories of growing up in hellish circumstances; of suffering sexual abuse and bullying and then, when it should have been all over, rampant discrimination from the states that had helped to put their parents away for the crimes they had committed. I became involved in creating a documentary, and in making a short film based on my life. The more I spoke, the more confident I became about having my voice heard. For a while, knowing that I was encouraging people to stand up for themselves, and not to feel ashamed about being who they are, became my reason for carrying on. I met a man called Brian Daniels, who owns a theatre in London, and was interested in giving the subject a forum in the theatre. When Brian and I attended a book launch together, I was introduced to Richard McCann, whose mother was the Yorkshire Ripper's first victim. Like me, Richard was determined for his story to be made public. I also met Bobbie-Louise Wilkinson, the daughter of Levi

Bellfield, the serial killer who was convicted of the murder of Millie Dowler, as well as a number of other girls and young women.

In early 2009, I did a radio interview with Claire Balding on Radio Five Live. Following this, my friend Brian and I attended a show at the Coliseum in Oldham, where I was introduced to the actress Claire Sweeney of *Brookside* fame. That Christmas, Tony and I, as well as his mother, went to the London Palladium to attend a charity event that had been set up to raise funds to keep Brian's theatre open. We had a fantastic time, met the cast of the 60-minute makeover show, and even saw Judge Judy, who was in the royal box. Michael Feinstein sang, and John Barrowman made a guest appearance. On another occasion, I met Sean Wilson, who was considering involvement in a theatre production about Richard McCann. Even in the glitzy world of show-business, people are fascinated with murder and mayhem. I couldn't get away from it. It was fascinating having a glimpse behind the scenes of show business, but what I gained most from the experience was a renewed sense of determination to tell my story and the story of all the innocent families of murderers, because ours are the voices that are seldom heard. I did my best to advocate for all the people in our situation. After a while, though, it became both tiring and lonely being the only voice speaking out. I needed to focus on myself for a while.

At home in my own community, I became deeply involved with a mental health charity. My colleagues knew what I had been through and were very supportive of me. I was very professional, and kept my work and my personal campaigns strictly separate. Once in a while, some of the exposure I received in the media attracted some negative attention, which we all ignored. Tony was busy too. He had attended an inspectors' course and had passed. It had been a difficult few years for us both. There were reports in the newspaper about my father being investigated for unsolved murders. Would I ever be able to close a door on my past? When the phone hacking scandal broke, and it was revealed that the *News of the World* had hacked the phones of dozens of people, including the families of murder victims, I worried that we had been hacked too. The *News of the World* had hounded us before and during the trial, and we had suspected at the time that our phones were bugged because the reception was so bad. The West Yorkshire Police helped us to get answers, and it seemed that we had not been implicated.

***

By 2011, my body could no longer cope with me burning the candle at both ends, and my health started to suffer. For months, I felt tired and run-down. I always seemed to have a cold or a sore throat. I tried to ignore the symptoms and just took more herbal supplements. I started to get a sharp pain under my right ribs, and brushed it off as the result of spending too much time at the gym. By November, I was looking forward to Christmas and working hard. I was sure that I'd feel better after the holidays.

On the 28th of November, I was busy in the office with a colleague, going through endless mounds of paperwork. At one point, my colleague left for the reception of the building. I hadn't noticed anyone coming in, and paid no attention. Then a former resident of the centre barged into the office together with his parents. I knew him because he had stayed with us before, and also because he remained in contact with a friend of his who was still living there. It quickly became apparent that he was unwell. Having grown up around people with mental health problems, and having worked in the area and trained to understand something about the issues, I felt that I was in a good position to deal with the situation and even defuse it. The man was getting agitated, and somebody needed to do something.

But no amount of training could have prepared me for what happened next. As if a switch had been flicked, the man rose from the chair he had taken and started to flail around wildly. He hit me a few times, and then moved on to my colleague, a woman. There was no way I was going to stand there and watch a man beat up a woman. No decent person would and, for me, having grown up watching my father beat my mother, it was unthinkable that I would stay still rather than get my colleague away from the man, who was clearly having a psychotic breakdown. By this stage, a number of the centre's residents had emerged from their rooms to see what was going on, and everyone was getting upset. Anyone who has ever worked in a psychiatric hospital will tell you that when a psychotic patient becomes violent, they display the strength of ten, and that when one mentally ill person in a facility kicks off, it can be so disturbing to the others that they quickly start becoming agitated too. That was certainly my experience.

We rang the police twice, and they eventually turned up. We had to implore them, but finally they agreed to take the man away. Later, I found out that they delivered him to the secure unit at the local hospital. After making sure that everyone in the building was OK, I collapsed. My colleague brought me to Accident and Emergency, where a chest x-ray revealed that my lungs were fine, but that I had numerous fractured ribs, as well as cuts and bruises.

I tried to return to work straight away, but it was too much for me, and I was signed off until early 2012 to give me time to heal. Over the course of the next eight weeks I was sore, suffered panic attacks at increasing intervals, and trusted nobody outside my home and family unit. Every time I left the house, I was sure the attacker would strike again. I started drinking to help myself calm down – not terrible binges, but up to a bottle of wine a day, which is a lot for me, and which didn't help at all.

With Tony's support, I made a statement to the Lancashire Police. I wanted to press charges, if only to ensure that the man who had attacked me was given the opportunity he needed to get better, and that he would not attack anyone else.

***

That Christmas, Dad managed to smuggle a card out of prison to be posted to my mother at Grandma's house.

"If you come to see me in jail," he wrote, "I'll tell you what happened on the day I took Lesley Molseed."

Dad went on to tell Mum that life was cushy in the prison. He was treated well, he said, the food was good, and the other prisoners even came to him for advice because they could see that he was an older, wiser man who knew a thing or two about life.

Mum was distraught. Just when she thought she had finally got him out of her life and could get on with living, Dad managed to taunt her, even from behind bars. She had been told that he would not be able to post letters to her, but he had foiled the system. I was furious. If he needed to unburden himself, why could he not at least tell Lesley Molseed's family the truth of what happened that day? Surely, he owed them, and the memory of the innocent man whose life was destroyed by his actions, some sort of explanation? I felt awful for Mum. All her married life, he had treated her with contempt, and brutalised her and her children. Why was he tormenting her now?

I felt even worse when I learned that Lancashire Police had never had any intention of pressing charges against my assailant, reasoning that the individual in question was mentally ill, and should have been dealt with within the mental health industry. The only bright light during this dark time was the fact that I celebrated my tenth anniversary with Tony in February. Tony arranged for us to spend a week in New York, where we saw all the sights. For a few days, I allowed myself to be happy. In general, however, unless I was with Tony, I didn't feel safe enough to leave the house. I was prescribed beta-blockers and attended intensive counselling sessions. Gradually, I started to talk about everything that happened to me during my childhood.

By May 2012, I had lodged an appeal requesting that the man who had attacked me be charged with the offence. I was in a relatively strong position, as I was in a civil partnership with a high-ranking officer, and was determined not to be brushed aside. I had already been in contact with the Ministry of Justice, and in contact with friends who work, respectively, as a solicitor and a judge. Just as before, I was determined that I should not be dismissed.

In the meantime, I was so preoccupied with achieving justice, I neglected my health even more. By June, I had started to pass blood in my stools and to experience horrible pain, fatigue, itchiness, and sweating. My doctor insisted that all the symptoms were psychosomatic because of the stress I had experienced since the attack, but finally agreed to refer me for an ultrasound, which revealed a swelling in the urinary system, and a deformation of the urethra. Further research has not explained why the swelling occurred and, in my wilder moments, I have wondered if it was God's way of punishing me for being the son of a murderer.

Despite all my efforts to escape from the stigma, I have had to accept that I am serving a life sentence after all. There are times when the fear and self-loathing recede, and then something happens, and it all comes flooding back. In the years since my father's trial, the media in Britain has been full of stories of child abuse. In the autumn of 2012, news broke of the abuse that had been committed by Britain's favourite eccentric, Jimmy Savile. Apparently, he had been abusing children for years. Everyone around him knew, to varying degrees, about his actions, and nobody said anything. I watched the news coverage of his victims explaining how they were full of shame. They had been taken for a ride in

Jimmy's Rolls Royce or brought to the BBC centre, where they had been abused. This was happening at the time when my father was fined £25 for an indecent assault on a child. When he was murdering Lesley Molseed. The children who survive abuse are filled with guilt. In the case of Savile's victims, because they had accepted the treats he offered, they felt complicit in what had happened to them. I know exactly how they feel, because that was just how it was for me, when I took money from my grandfather after he abused me. I wonder what would have happened, back then, if I had told someone about what was happening. Quite likely, I would not have been believed. What would have happened, if my father had been properly investigated after being convicted of assault in 1976 and paying a £25 fine?

In November 2012, the newspapers broke the story that the rumours that had long circulated about Cyril Smith, MP, were true: like Jimmy Savile, he had been a serial child abuser of long standing. Given his close relationship with my grandfather, and the fact that my grandfather abused me, I worry that yet more revelations about my family will come to light. As part of the police investigation into the posthumous accusations against Smith, I was interviewed for whatever I could tell them about his relationship with my family. I will never know for sure, but all the evidence suggests that both my grandfather and my father were involved in a paedophile ring that also included Cyril Smith. I am sure that there are many more victims than we'll ever know about. I was silent for years about what I had been through; there may be scores of abuse victims of my grandfather and father who have not yet spoken out.

I presume that my father was abused by his father, and that this is how he learned the behaviour that led him to become a child killer; that doesn't excuse, but might help explain, his own actions as an adult. Given what I now know about my father, I am tormented by the thought that he probably molested, and maybe even killed, more children. I have asked him to see me to answer my questions, but he has refused to do even that. I have never understood why he hates me so much.

Whenever I think that it's over, that I am finally going to be able to put it all behind me, something else happens. Whenever I read newspaper reports about murderers, it brings everything back. In October 2012, I read an interview with a woman called Karen Edwards, whose daughter Becky was murdered by a man called Christopher Halliwell. Just as the Molseeds said of us, she stated that she has never blamed Becky's killer's family, whom she met during the trial; that she sees that they are his victims just as she is. When I encounter such kindness and generosity of spirit, it moves me deeply. I hope for the day when Mum and Karen, my father's second wife, can come together in public and show, through their unity, that even far-flung families can come together to denounce the killers in their midst, support each other, and show the world that they are not to blame for what has happened.

In 2014, my father tried to get in contact. He had sent a letter to Mum's house, and one to me, having found out my address via a solicitor. As I knew by now that he had no intention of being honest with me, I didn't want to hear from him. Mum and I contacted the jail and asked them to ensure that he was not allowed to send us any mail. They were not very cooperative, and told me that they could not control everything he did. I persisted, putting it in writing that we did not want to receive any letters from him. I had to return Dad's letter to them as proof that he had been bothering me.

That same year, I decided that I had been dealing with Dad for long enough. The problem was that every time someone Googled his name, mine came up too. I decided to contact Google to arrange to have any articles mentioning me removed from their database. A number of people had read about the case and had subsequently looked me up on Facebook to send me messages. Most of the messages were complimentary, but it was still more than I could cope with, and I knew that I needed to restore my privacy. It was amazingly easy dealing with Google, and all the articles discussing me were gone within a couple of weeks. The local papers contacted me to see if I had any comment on my father's right to be forgotten. I said, "No comment." I knew that it was upsetting for the Molseeds to have much of the commentary about the case removed from the Internet, but I want them to know that it was nothing to do with Dad, but about my own need for privacy and the right to move on with my life.

People often fret about the human rights of people who are spending time behind bars for the terrible crimes that they have committed. I wonder if those people ever think about the human rights of the unhappy families left behind, both the bereaved and the families of the murderers, who never manage to live down their shame for something that is not their fault. I am still sometimes asked to give interviews in the media, often together with other family members of convicted killers. While I do believe that it is crucial that our voices be heard, I have realised that the shows' directors don't understand, or possibly don't care, that these appearances can bring back pain and distress that we need to move away from. I know now that the one thing that helps victims of sexual and physical abuse is the ability to tell someone else, and ease their psychological burden, but that the best forum is not a television show.

It's common knowledge that many abusers were abused as children themselves, but not so well-known that the vast majority of abuse victims never commit such crimes. Strange as it seems, accepting that some people will always see me as a murderer's son and nothing else has given me some release. After all, there's a limit to how much I can change other people's minds. All I can do is my best. I am sometimes tempted to drink too much, but I focus on getting plenty of exercise and releasing feel-good endorphins that way, instead. There are times when I feel immersed in anger, bitterness, and shame – but when that happens, I remind myself of how lucky I really am. I live in a beautiful home with a wonderful man who loves me, and who has given me opportunities and confidence I never experienced before meeting him. For the son of a murderer, who grew up in an abusive home and left school with no qualifications, I suppose I've done all right.

***

In 2014, same-sex marriage was finally legalised in England and Wales, and by the following year I had decided that it was time to get married. We already had a civil partnership, but I wanted all the rights that go with marriage, as well as the opportunity to stand up with the man I love before the people I care about and pledge my life to him without reservation. Tony and I were spending the day at a spa and I had everything planned: I made an excuse to go upstairs and reserve a table, and on the way, I talked to the maître d' and asked him to come out after the first course with a tray of champagne and an engagement ring. The waiter came out with the tray, and while Tony turned around to take his glass, I got down on one knee and proposed. The normally phlegmatic Tony was tearful and excited, and four months later we had the wedding of our dreams in a beautiful country hotel, replete with a mist machine, topless waiters (a couple of guys I know from the gym) and all the works. We celebrated in front of all our closest friends and, finally, I felt that I had laid my ghosts to rest. The news that our dream wedding would be featured in a magazine was the icing on the cake.

All my life, all I ever wanted was for a kind man, a bit older than me, to fall in love with me and promise to take care of me. In Tony, all my dreams had come true. Our relationship is completely unlike Mum and Dad's. We share the housework and cooking, and we support one another. When Tony has a long shift, I am the one who takes the dogs for a walk, gets the shopping in, and makes sure that the house is clean, and when I am the one who is busy, Tony does the same for me.

At last, I felt ready to really grow up and become a dad. Tony and I started the proceedings to adopt a child, determined that our son will have the happy childhood that I never did, and that Lesley Molseed had taken from her.

Postscript

Dad has continued to write countless letters to Mum, claiming that he has been the victim of a miscarriage of justice, and that he needs her to support him in a campaign for his freedom. Jason believes him and continues to visit, but Mum knows that he is guilty and wants nothing to do with him. Jason is still so angry with us for testifying against Dad that he has cut off all contact, and Mum does not even know her own grandchildren, which is a constant cause of sorrow to her. I wish Jason and his family all the best, but I accept his decision, and I hope that one day he will be able to see our father for the monster that he is.

Dad continued to try to contact me for a period of time. He has written to me saying that he forgives me and hoping that we can rebuild a relationship. I have no interest in ever communicating with him again and, in fact, Tony and I are prohibited from doing so, as we are becoming adoptive parents. However, some years ago, I rang the prison to request a visiting order, only for Dad to refuse to issue one. I wanted to confront him for one last time, and perhaps to hear him admit at least some of the things that he has done. I know that he will never admit to murdering Lesley, but I would have liked to hear him attempt to justify his behaviour towards me. The reality is that he is only interested in communicating with me on his own terms, and those are terms that I am not prepared to accept. I often wonder why, considering his age and the fact that he is not in the best of health, Dad doesn't admit what he has done, and try to find some peace in accepting that he is guilty and is being punished. Perhaps he simply spent so long living a double life that that is all he knows.

The damage my father did to his family has never really been repaired. I would like to report that my mother and I became close after the trial but, although I will always love her, that never happened. She chose not to get the psychological support she needed, and she and Daniel have retreated into a miserable life of their own making. Daniel is a talented man, capable of achieving great things, but he has never worked. Benefits have become a way of life for them both. They do not take care of themselves, and their health has suffered in consequence. Food has become a comfort to them, and they both struggle badly with their weight. Like so many, they are caught in a poverty trap, unable to afford a good diet on a low income, with the temptation of resorting to empty calories in return for short term rewards. They still live in the town where I grew up, and where Dad carried out his dreadful crime. They have no friends, and are often bullied and teased by their neighbours because they stand out as being odd and different, and because of the taint of their association with Dad. I have tried to remind Daniel that Mum won't always be there, and that it is important for him to build some sort of a life for himself, but the world is a difficult place for him. Daniel now manipulates Mum, and she has fallen into her old role of appeaser and subject. He manages their small income and decides how it will be spent, and he decides who is and who is not welcome to visit them in their home. I had hoped that they would move on and find happiness, but Dad destroyed their confidence to the extent that it seems like they will never get it back.

I asked Mum if she would have stayed with Dad, knowing what he had done.

"I don't know," she said. "Where would I have gone? I had no money and three children."

Without a job, Mum would have struggled badly on leaving the father of her children. Women who give up work completely, and rely on a man to support them, are in an extremely vulnerable situation. From witnessing my mother's experience, I have learned how important it is for women to retain their independence. The advice that I would give to any young wife and mother is to keep working, at least part time, to retain the skills and connections that will enable her to make it on her own if that ever becomes necessary.

I do still struggle to accept that my mother stayed with my father despite his actions. She did not know about his paedophilia, although she did give evidence in his support when he was convicted of molesting a child, but she did know that he had been involved in a robbery. She certainly knew that he mistreated all his children very badly. Because she had become dependent on him, it never really occurred to her that she could leave.

As more and more news breaks about paedophiles, including organised paedophile rings, I feel sure that the full story of my father's activities has not yet been told. Clearly, the fact that my abusive grandfather and father were friendly with the paedophile MP Cyril Smith is at least suggestive of the possibility that all three were members of a group with an interest in victimising and molesting children. The wider Rochdale area has seen horrendous levels of sexual abuse, and I am confident that my older male relatives contributed much of it. Mum clearly remembers the names and faces of many of the friends and acquaintances of Cyril Smith and my grandfather, and she has given this information to the police but, to the best of my knowledge, few, if any, of them have been prosecuted. The sad reality is that sexual crimes against children and other vulnerable members of society were not investigated as carefully as they should have been in the 1970s. On the one hand, the testimony of girls and women – and of gay men – was often dismissed by a biased police force, while on the other, I believe that powerful men like Cyril Smith had the means and the opportunity to bribe and pay their way out of difficult circumstances. It is a matter of public record that Stefan Kiszko's mother directly approached Cyril Smith and asked him for help, and that he ignored her. It is not a great stretch of the imagination to wonder if my father's parents, his close friends, knew or suspected what their then young son had done, and asked him for help. Given that my grandfather was a convicted sexual abuser, and my grandparents' long history of easing my father's path through life with their money, I believe that they used their connections in government and in local circles of influence to protect my father and prevent the Molseed family from obtaining justice. The penalties my father received for molesting other children were pitifully small, even by the standards of the day, and I suspect that the families in question – poor and easily swayed by more influential members of their community – must have been paid off. In court, it emerged that Dad had received psychiatric care when he was twenty-one, after murdering Lesley Molseed. I believe that his parents knew very well what he had done and urged him to stay with Mum, who had just borne another man's child, so that he would look less like a murderer. It was already too late for Lesley, but I wonder why they did not ensure that he got the help he needed not to feel the desire to hurt and brutalise his own family, too. My grandfather continued to speak well of Cyril Smith until the day I found him naked and dead on his bathroom floor. I will never know for sure what secrets they shared, but I do know that money can do anything.

A simple truth that I continue to struggle with is the fact that I owe my existence to my father's aberrant sexual tastes. Because his interest was in pre-teens, he had a great need to appear to the world to be a normal, ordinary family man. For this reason, he looked for and found my mother, Beverly. He made her dependent on him by insisting that she give up work and devote her life to her family, and by grinding her down so much that her already low self-esteem was completely destroyed. That is why he accepted the presence of Jason in his family, even though Jason had a different biological father, and why both Daniel and I were born. We were his façade. He never cared about any of us except insofar as our existence made it easier for him to continue with his aberrant behaviour. In retrospect, I can see that the memory of what he did to Lesley haunted Dad every day of his life. He lived with the fear of being found out. That fear led him to marry a woman he clearly despised, and to have children he never wanted or liked. It led him to buy guns to protect himself from imaginary assailants.

I rarely visit my hometown. There are too many painful memories, and it is difficult seeing people I remember from my childhood crossing the road to avoid me because they don't know what to say. There are some who make a point of coming up to me, putting an arm around me, and telling me that I am looking well, and that they are happy to see that my life has worked out. I will always appreciate their support. Once in a while, wandering around the supermarket or on the street, I have seen parents of my childhood friends, such as Elizabeth's family. We smile and nod, and move on with our shopping trolleys. Sometimes I think about going up to them, striking up a conversation, and trying to reconnect, but too much time has passed, and too many things have changed. I just hope they know that they made a positive difference for me when I was a damaged little boy. On a number of occasions, I have bumped into the boys – now men – who bullied me and made my life an absolute misery as a child. It is to the credit of some of them that they have come up to me and apologised for their behaviour back then.

I am blessed in having found Tony. With his support, I have been able to conquer the OCD that, at one time, seemed like it was going to destroy my life, and I have seen my self-esteem flourish. At the time of writing, Tony and I are about to adopt a little boy and become parents together for the first time. I long ago ruled out the possibility of ever having a biological child, because of my concerns that some rogue gene, handed down from my father, might once again be manifested in a devastating way. While this is an extremely happy time in our lives, I do worry about how I will address the matter of my father and his crimes with our son as he grows up. At some point, he will notice that there are no photographs of my family in the house, and he may ask why. Will I have to tell him the truth? We are blessed to have

Tony's family, who will welcome our child into their hearts and provide him with a ready-made assortment of uncles, aunts, and cousins. While I wish that my family could do the same, that will never be possible. The wedge that my father drove between us is simply too great.

To anyone who has suffered an abusive childhood, an abusive marriage, or sexual assault or abuse, I would say, speak out and get help. Go to counselling. Tell the people you love and trust. Do whatever it takes to get to the root of the things that trouble you, because when you understand yourself better, you can start to heal. To those in a situation like mine, struggling to cope with the knowledge that their parent is an abuser or a killer, I would like to say that you are not alone. Sadly, there are far more of us than anyone could imagine. Whatever your father or mother did, it is not your fault, and the best way you can repay society for crimes that were not committed by you is to go on and have a happy, fulfilled life, to be kind to everyone you encounter, and to make sure that you do not allow them to destroy your life as they have destroyed others'. You are a victim too, but with time, love, and support, you can become a survivor.

I would like the Molseed family to know that although Lesley was murdered before I was born, I think of her every day. All these years later, there is nothing I can do to comfort the Molseeds, but I can make sure that my own child grows up with the love and guidance that my father never gave me, and I can ensure that he is taught to respect others as he would like to be respected, regardless of who or what they are. I can work every day to give him the sort of upbringing that I never had. When he grows up, I hope that he will enjoy the many things that were stolen by my father from Lesley Molseed – romantic love, marriage, education, and opportunity. When he is old enough, I will tell him about her, so that he can remember her too.

Printed in Great Britain
by Amazon

29231392R00118